Michael Perham is the Bishop of Gloucester and was an architect of *Common Worship*. He is the author of many books, including most recently *New Handbook of Pastoral Liturgy*, a guide using *Common Worship* liturgies, and *Signs of Your Kingdom*.

GW00359326

GLORY IN
OUR MIDST

Michael Perham

First published in Great Britain in 2005

Society for Promoting Christian Knowledge
36 Causton Street
London SW1P 4ST

British Library Cataloguing-in-Publication Data
A catalogue record for this book is available from the British Library

ISBN 0–281–05582–3

1 3 5 7 9 10 8 6 4 2

Typeset by Kenneth Burnley, Wirral, Cheshire
Printed in Great Britain by Bookmarque

All honour and praise be yours always and everywhere,
mighty creator, ever-living God,
through Jesus Christ your only Son our Lord:
for at this time we celebrate your glory
made present in our midst.

Epiphany Preface,
Common Worship

For the Chapter and Congregation
of Derby Cathedral
among whom I was privileged to minister
from 1998 to 2004

Contents

———◆◆◆———

Preface

Glory in Our Midst treats the period from the beginning of Advent to the very end of Christmas and Epiphany at Candlemas as a unity and explores how, gradually, the meaning of Christ's coming is revealed and how, behind that unfolding, there emerge key elements in the Christian understanding of God himself.

This is a book that one could sit down and read at a single long sitting at any stage through December and January as Advent gives way to Christmas and Christmas to Epiphany. But I have imagined it as a book that some will choose to read, chapter by chapter, through the ten weeks from Advent to Candlemas, and I have therefore ensured that, though chapters are not allocated to particular days, there is sufficient material to read in each season. There is a chapter a week and a little more. There is an overall theme and development from one chapter to another. Nevertheless, each chapter stands on its own as an independent unit.

Some chapters are entirely newly written; others had their origin in sermons or addresses in Norwich, Derby or Gloucester. I am grateful to the communities that stimulated the thinking that led to the first drafts of some of the material in the book, not least to my former colleagues in the Chapter at Derby Cathedral and to the congregation there. I dedicate *Glory in Our Midst* to them with gratitude and affection.

I am aware that, as well as scripture and my own reflections upon it, there is also a good deal of the writing of theologians and poets whose work has inspired and challenged me. I have returned, as I frequently do, to the poetry of T. S. Eliot, Elizabeth Jennings and Edwin le Grice. I am also aware of how much I have been learning from the material from the Fathers that Robert Atwell includes in *Celebrating the Saints* and *Celebrating the Seasons*. He inspires me to go back to the sources when space for study allows and meanwhile provides me with much food for reflection through his well-chosen selection.

Preface

I am, as always, grateful to the publishing staff at SPCK, who have published all the books I have written over more than 25 years, and especially to Joanna Moriarty, who has been both helpful and encouraging in the writing of *Glory in Our Midst*.

For me, the weeks from Advent to Candlemas are full of delight. The biblical stories they recall are full of fascination, the liturgy of the seasons is rich and many-layered, and the theological truths about the one whose glory is in our midst are exciting to share. Good news always needs to be proclaimed.

✠ *Michael Gloucestr:*
Gloucester

ADVENT

1

He comes, both Child and Judge

The First Sunday of Advent is always a new beginning. You can make too much of the idea of the start of the Church's new year, for in a cycle there is, in a sense, no end and no beginning, and the ideas that are in the air in November of Christ, his kingdom and the commun-ion of his saints all anticipate the themes that Advent will explore. Nevertheless, Advent does have the element of the fresh start, the beginning of a series of units of time that will bring us in due course to the Presentation of Christ in the Temple, some nine weeks on at the beginning of February. At least that is the way it can be and, if it is understood like that, it can be an enriching experience as Advent gives way to Christmas, Christmas to Epiphany and Epiphany to Candlemas. Each unit is different, but they belong together as, little by little, they unfold for us the glory in our midst and reveal at least something of what we mean when we say that God is with us – *Emmanuel.*

Advent has a mood all of its own, with its distinctive hymns, its wreath waiting to be lit each week, its hint of something different in the air, something solemn yet joyful just around the corner. It is one of those subtle seasons, where things go on at different levels and where it is easy to miss the deeper levels altogether.

Advent is about coming. It is, for most, about the coming of Christmas, a sort of religious dimension to the frantic preparations to be ready for 25 December. Christians might prefer to say, not so much that it is about the coming of Christmas, but about the coming of Christ, recognizing that part of what we are trying to do is to enter sufficiently into the mystery of the incarnation that, in a sense, Christ is born all over again, that he really comes and makes his home within us. 'Be born in us today' we sing at Christmas, and our hope

3

is that they will not be empty words, but a real longing for Christ to find his home within us.

Yet, of course, at another level, Advent is not about that coming at all – long ago, or even made present in us now – but about a future coming, a coming at the end of time. The Advent hymns that people delight to sing are nearly all about that coming on the clouds of heaven, the sort of end-of-time events that the evangelists write about:

> two will be in the field; one will be taken, and one will be left. Two women will be grinding meal together; one will be taken and one will be left. Keep awake, therefore, for you do not know on what day your Lord is coming . . . for the Son of Man is coming at an unexpected hour.
>
> (Matthew 24.40–42, 44)

When Charles Wesley wrote in the eighteenth century

> Lo! He comes with clouds descending,
> Once for favoured sinners slain;
> Thousand thousand saints attending
> Swell the triumph of his train;
> Alleluia! Alleluia!
> God appears on earth to reign

it was to a second coming that he was pointing.

The truth is that the Advent emphasis on a second coming is often squeezed out by other preoccupations. Pre-Christmas preparation and even festivity can mean that the Advent themes have little chance to make their impact. Ann Lewin expresses it like this in a poem entitled 'Wachet Auf':

> Advent.
> Season when
> Dual citizenship
> Holds us in awkward tension.
>
> The world, intent on
> Spending Christmas,
> Eats and drinks its way to
> Oblivion after dinner.
> The kingdom sounds
> Insistent warnings:

Repent, be ready,
Keep awake,
He comes.

Like some great fugue
The themes entwine:
The Christmas carols,
Demanding our attention
In shops and pubs,
Bore their insistent way
Through noise of traffic;
Underneath, almost unheard,
The steady solemn theme of
Advent.

With growing complexity,
Clashing, blending,
Rivals for our attention,
Themes mingle and separate,
Pulling us with increasing
Urgency,
Until in final resolution,
The end attained,
Harmony rests in aweful
Stillness, and
The child is born.

He comes,
Both Child and Judge.

And will he find us
Watching?
(From *Watching for the Kingfisher*)

But the truth is that Christians are sometimes happy enough to see
Advent squeezed and its themes neglected. It is not simply that we
enjoy getting into Christmas long before 25 December, but because
the traditional Advent imagery – the end of the world, the coming of
Christ to judge, the final consummation – puzzles us profoundly.
We ask ourselves whether we really expect these things to happen.
If we can make sense at all of assertions such as 'Christ will come
again', is it only by investing them with meaning very different from

their plain original sense? The second coming is for many Christians an embarrassment and the invitation in the Advent hymns to the Lord to return is not one they expect to find accepted.

Here is an area of real theological perplexity for us. It is clear that for Jesus, especially as Matthew and Mark portray him, theology was eschatology, or, putting it more simply, to talk of God was to talk of the imminent coming kingdom that would sweep away the current world order. He saw his own life as the breaking in of that kingdom and his death as part of a final struggle. The disciples must keep awake and be ready, lest they be unprepared when the end of the world order came. Nor was this belief of his, that comes out so clearly in his teaching, among the more peripheral parts of his message. The *parousia*, to use the technical term for the second coming, was central to his thinking. It shaped many elements of his attitudes and teachings. It was, you might say, a central plank of his theology.

Nor was it Jesus alone who saw things in this way. The first Christians shared this view that the end was near. They had no long-term strategy for God's mission in the world, for the world was perishing. They had an immediate urgent message for a world that was passing away. The apostle Paul shared this view, and his advice and teaching about ethical matters was based on the assumption that they were living in the last times. His earliest letters have a great urgency about them; the later ones begin to recognize a different time-scale before the end.

Our Christian forebears learnt to modify the New Testament picture as each generation succeeded another and the end did not come. Nevertheless, however long delayed, the day of reckoning would surely come. Our medieval churches, in their paintings, proclaimed more than anything else the final judgement and the division of the sheep and the goats, the saved and the damned. This emphasis on the end has always been an important strand of the Christian tradition.

But what of today? Do Christians believe – are Christians required to believe – that God will intervene to bring the created order to an end? And, if they do believe that, do they seriously allow for the possibility that that intervention might come at any moment? If they speak of a cataclysmic end, is it not one they envisage will be brought about by the human race in its foolishness, through weapons of global destruction or environmental folly, rather than divine intervention? And, if they do envisage it, do they not fear it, rather than yearn for it, and look forward to it in the way the first Christians did? What do they make of those who stand in city centres with their sandwich boards proclaiming a biblical message about the end? Are they not embarrassed by those who take the scriptures with the utmost seriousness?

Like many Christians, I live with a dilemma. I cannot entirely make sense of the end-of-time language of the New Testament and certainly cannot sort out the truth from the pictorial language in which it is expressed. Yet I am deeply unhappy with attempts to reinterpret such language out of existence. I would fight hard against any attempt to abandon this world of eschatology. I would rather cling on to these concepts, of which I cannot entirely make sense, than try to envisage a Christianity without them. I need to go on saying, like the first Christians in their Aramaic acclamation, *Maranatha*, 'The Lord is coming.'

That is not just because such belief is central to scripture, though it is, and that alone means that I need to take it very seriously. Nor is it only because such belief is central to Jesus's thinking, though I do not know how you can begin to understand him without taking on board something that motivated him so profoundly. Nor, in the end, is it because a faith that has jettisoned the second coming might be a more comfortable and cosy religion, without much guts – though that is an important consideration, for a Christianity without the judgement seat of Christ loses a proper corrective to the picture of an all-embracing love upon the cross.

No, in the end, I believe we must go on expressing our faith through the language of second coming, judgement and end of time for two reasons: it is the only language we have to enshrine and protect an important truth, and it is the only language we have to give urgency to our proclamation.

The truth that it enshrines and protects is the social character of salvation. The scriptures have little interest in you and me finding salvation, reaching perfection, being drawn into heaven (and we can express it in several ways) on our own. They attach very little importance to the moment of death and certainly do not identify it with the time of judgement. There is a wonderful and crucial truth hidden in a line in one of Michel Quoist's prayers, 'I cannot save myself alone.' My salvation, my perfection, my endless joy and felicity, cannot be in isolation from everybody else's. All that end-of-the-world talk addresses that. It affirms that God wants to bring everything together, to put in the last pieces of the jigsaw, to complete the grand design, to put everybody and everything in its proper place. It is a picture in which I fulfil my eternal destiny in solidarity with all my brothers and sisters. It is a final consummation, in which all shall be well for the elect of God.

Of course there is a personal element to it. To some extent I have to stand alone and face my creator and my saviour – not as some private or individual encounter, but because he is bringing everything to completion and to wholeness. An event in which the totality of human history is brought to the throne of God demands strong, poetic, cosmic images, and the language of eschatology meets that need. So, yes, I can say *Maranatha*, 'The Lord is coming', and pray 'Come, Lord Jesus, and touch the whole world.'

Though I think the language of the end of time is essentially the language of artist and poet, I believe that the action of the creator God will be at work when, for whatever scientific reason, this planet of ours comes to an end. I respond to the picture that Pierre Teilhard de Chardin, with his scientific mind, paints.

> One day, the gospel tells us, the tension gradually accumulating between humanity and God will touch the limits prescribed by the possibilities of the world. And then will come the end. Then the presence of Christ which has been silently accruing in things, will suddenly be revealed – like a flash of light from pole to pole. Breaking through all the barriers within which the veil of matter and the water-tightness of souls have seemingly kept it confined, it will invade the face of the earth.
>
> (*Le Milieu Divin*)

Yes, Christ will come again.

But the language of the end also gives urgency to our proclamation. One of the things that followed from a belief that the end was near – it comes in the middle of the night like a thief at any moment – was a marvellous urgency to proclaim the good news and to draw men and women into the kingdom while there was still time. Yet we act, individually and as the Church, as if we had all the time in the world, and I suppose we think we have. The Church grew quickly, the faith spread effectively, where Christians believed the end was around the corner. The Church made less impact, the proclamation weakened, when there was always tomorrow to spread the gospel. Part of the challenge of Advent is to recover that divine urgency that marked the whirlwind ministry of Jesus and the irrepressible need to tell that characterized the early Church. We need to hear Jesus saying, 'I am coming quickly, I am coming soon', not because we can predict from that when the end will come – as if we could begin to understand the mystery of time in relation to God's eternity – but because we need to be encouraged to be urgent in our proclamation of the gospel. I want to have reinforced for me the challenge to preach the good news, in season and out of season, persuasively, joyfully and urgently, as if there were no tomorrow.

This end-of-time dimension inevitably shapes the character of Advent. I identify three particular marks of Advent that arise if one takes seriously a second coming as much as a first.

The first is expectancy. The traditional word is 'hope', but that word has become so enfeebled in our vocabulary that the stronger word, 'expectancy', is more helpful. There is that wonderful sentence in Luke's account of the ministry of John the Baptist which one version translates 'The people were on the tiptoe of expectation' (Luke 3.15, NEB). That is the meaning of Christian hope, an urgent yet confident expectation. The Advent readings from the prophets are full of it, as in the future tenses about what the Lord will do when the shoot shall come from the stock of Jesse.

> He shall judge the poor, and decide with equity for the meek of the earth; he shall strike the earth with the rod of his mouth . . . The wolf shall live with the lamb, the leopard shall lie down with the kid . . . They will not hurt or destroy on all my holy mountain; for the earth will be full of the knowledge of the LORD as the waters cover the sea.
>
> (Isaiah 11.4, 6, 9)

This urgent and confident expectation is a belief that God is a God who acts, who acted in Jesus, and who can and will act in you and me. We have grown too used to the idea that God's activity is in the past tense, that we simply recall and remember his mighty acts. But Christian hope insists, 'No, he is acting now. Don't close your eyes for a single moment lest you miss some fresh outburst of his activity, some new impact of the divine upon the world. Be awake! Be alert! Be expectant!'

But a second mark of Advent is struggle. In particular there is the struggle to discern God's word for us. Of course that is a task laid upon the Christian in every season, but Advent presents us with it in two particular ways. First, there is the rich treasury of prophecy that the Church encourages us to read in the season of Advent, ancient Old Testament prophecies that, whatever their original meaning, later generations interpreted as prefiguring the birth of Jesus. Second, there are the very testing passages in the New Testament that, as we have seen already, speak of the end of the world, the second coming and the judgement seat of God.

That is the word of God for us in scripture, which is our primary source. But the word of God for us comes in a variety of ways, and making sense of its sheer diversity does involve struggle for the serious seeker after truth. Supremely, of course, the word of God jumps out at us from the pages of the Bible. But it comes also through the tradition of the Church, itself a fragile and sensitive thing, sometimes apparently contradictory, sometimes a reassuring protection from frightening innovation, sometimes a constricting straitjacket that seems to hold us back. Yet scripture and tradition are not the sum total of the ways in which God seems to be speaking to us. He speaks also in fresh and disturbing ways in the Church of our own day. His Spirit often seems to be challenging our old assumptions and calling us to be thinking again. Only the very frightened will fail to acknowledge that, behind the wind of change blowing through the Church, there is something of the Spirit of God.

But God also speaks outside the Church. He seems to be telling us things through nature, through art, through history, through the events of our time, through our neighbours. And besides all that – which is, in a sense, outside and around us, impinging on us – there is a voice of God within, a reason and a conscience, often confused, sometimes at odds with the accepted view, puzzled and perplexed. A voice within, and so many voices, apparently contradictory, without – and all, in some measure, means by which God's word for us may be apprehended and received. Making sense of that is a struggle. The urgent expectation of Advent is not just frothy excitement, but a deeply serious searching.

The third mark of Advent is repentance. It is not a season of repentance in quite the way that Lent is, but repentance is nevertheless very much part of the Advent story, not only because it is a proper response to a Christ who will come in judgement at the end of time, but also because of the strange and disturbing figure of John the Baptist who is soon on the Advent stage with his unpalatable opening speech, 'Repent, for the kingdom of heaven is at hand' and his call to 'bear fruit worthy of repentance'. With John and with repentance, a third mark of Advent, the two following chapters engage.

Advent teaches us that to find Jesus is not just to find a baby in a manger. The baby is part of the truth of the glory in our midst, but there is more to be said and more to be known. It teaches us that to find Jesus is to find the one who, for all his love and his mercy, is judge. In Anne Lewin's phrase, 'he comes, both Child and Judge'. Advent signals that at the beginning of this succession of seasons, just as Candlemas will herald it at the end. 'The Lord whom you seek will suddenly come to his temple. The messenger of the covenant in whom you delight – indeed, he is coming, says the LORD of hosts. But who can endure the day of his coming, and who can stand when he appears?' (Malachi 3.1–2). It teaches us that to find Jesus, the supreme Word of the Father, we need to engage with his word for us that comes in so many different ways, often through search and struggle. It teaches us that to find Jesus, and to reveal him to others, has an urgency about it, as if there were no tomorrow. Advent teaches us that there may already be glory in our midst, but in the plan of God there is more glory still to come. The world has not seen the last of Jesus.

2

See the glory, wear the glory

————◆————

Saint John:
you are the John that baptized God;
you were praised by an archangel
before you were begotten by your father;
you were full of God before you were born of your mother;
you knew God before you knew the world;
you showed your mother the mother bearing God
before the mother who bore you within her
showed you the day.
It was of you that God said:
'Among them that are born of women
there has not arisen a greater.'
To you, sir, who are so great, holy and blessed,
comes a guilty, creeping thing, a wretched little man,
whose senses are almost dead with grief . . .
to you, so great a friend of God.
(Benedicta Ward, *The Prayers and Meditations of St Anselm*)

Thus Anselm, the great twelfth-century theologian and archbishop, begins his long prayer to St John the Baptist, in which he explores John's closeness to Christ and to God.

We are not far into Advent before the figure of John the Baptist appears on the horizon. Not surprisingly so, if Advent is a time of new beginnings, for the Gospel writers are also quick to introduce him, Mark right at the beginning, Matthew once the stories of the birth of Jesus have been told, and John only a few verses into his prologue. Soon on the scene is the disconcerting wild man from the desert.

Of course that is not how Luke first introduces him. He tells in chapter 1 of his Gospel the wondrous tale of the announcement by the angel Gabriel to his father Zechariah in the temple that John was to be born, despite the old age of his parents. He goes on to tell how that birth took place and how Zechariah, who had been struck dumb, suddenly found his voice, confirmed 'His name is John' and took off into his great song of praise, which the Church has named *Benedictus* and incorporated into its worship each morning as the Gospel canticle at Morning Prayer:

> Blessed be the Lord God of Israel,
> who has come to his people and set them free.
> He has raised up for us a mighty Saviour;
> born of the house of his servant David . . .
> And you, child, shall be called the prophet of the Most High,
> for you will go before the Lord to prepare his way.
>
> (Luke 1.68–69, 76)

Yet, attractive as those stories of the annunciation to Zechariah and the birth of John are, the Church shows little interest in them in Advent, but focuses instead on the grown-up John, crying in the wilderness, 'Prepare the way of the Lord.' It pictures him standing by the Jordan proclaiming a baptism of repentance for the forgiveness of sins.

John is a striking and puzzling figure. He seems almost to come out of nowhere. The word of the Lord came to him in the wilderness, a lone voice in the desert. Certainly as Matthew and Mark tell it, that is the first we hear of him. He is an awkward prophetic figure with an unpalatable message delivered in an uncompromising style. But, of course, as Luke tells it, he does not come from nowhere. He comes from a priestly family. He comes of pious parents. Augustine of Hippo observes that

> John marks the boundary between the Old and New Testaments. Indeed the Lord speaks of him as a sort of boundary line, when he says that 'the Law and the prophets are valid until John the Baptist'. John is both the representative of the past and the herald of the new. As a representative of the past, it was fitting that he should have been born of elderly parents; and yet while still in his mother's womb he was declared to be a prophet in recognition of his future role. (Sermon 293, 1–3, in Robert Atwell,
> *Celebrating the Saints*)

I do not think it is unimportant that it was in the temple that the message of Gabriel is delivered. Old Zechariah is ministering in the temple and presenting the incense offering. Into this priestly setting, when Zechariah is fulfilling his ministry, creating a sense of worship so that the people may draw close to God, comes the message of the birth of the one who is to be a prophet. Into my mind comes the story of the call of that earlier prophet Isaiah, who, likewise, was in the temple when the call came.

> I saw the Lord sitting on a throne, high and lofty; and the hem of his robe filled the temple. Seraphs were in attendance above him; each had six wings: with two they covered their faces, and with two they covered their feet, and with two they flew. And one called to another and said: 'Holy, holy, holy is the LORD of hosts; the whole earth is full of his glory.'
>
> (Isaiah 6.1–3)

The incense was apparent then also, for we are told 'the house was filled with smoke'. Isaiah was a prophet drawn out of priestliness; so was John. For the passionate sense of God's justice that often marks the prophet is frequently born of the experience of God's holiness that the priest is called to reflect and to proclaim.

John's great call is the call to repentance, to fresh direction, to new start. But the call to repentance hardly ever comes from nowhere – no more than John himself comes from nowhere. The call to repentance comes from a deep sense of the holiness of God. It is when we see ourselves up against the glory of God, the sheer holiness, the uncompromisable justice, that we are brought to the point of crisis. In the end people are not challenged so much by commandments or by pleas for reform, but by encounter with the unutterable beauty, glory, holiness and justice of God, which shows us up for what we are, and our shoddiness and sinfulness for what they are. There is a direct relationship between the visions of Isaiah and Zechariah in the temple and the call to repentance of the wild man by the Jordan.

There is a lovely passage in the Book of Baruch (one of the so-called Apocryphal books), often read in Advent, that helps to illuminate this. 'Take off the garment of your sorrow and affliction, O Jerusalem', says Baruch,

and put on for ever the beauty of the glory from God.
Put on the robe of righteousness that comes from God;
put on your head the diadem of the glory of the Everlasting;
for God will show your splendour everywhere under heaven.
For God will give you evermore the name,
'Righteous Peace, Godly Glory.'

(Baruch 5.1–4)

For it is when we come to see the glory that we find ourselves swept off our feet or brought to our knees or blinded by the sheer light, as happened to Paul on the Damascus road. It is that vision of the glory that brings us to repentance.

There is a fine prayer by Archbishop William Temple that helps us see how repentance emerges from the vision of God. It has an Advent ring to it.

God, our Judge and Saviour,
set before us the vision of your purity,
and let us see our sins in the light of your holiness.
Pierce our self-contentment
with the shafts of your burning love,
and let that love consume all that hinders us
from perfect service of your cause;
for as your holiness is our judgement,
so are your wounds our salvation.
(In David Silk, *Prayers for Use at the Alternative Services*)

So, in a sense, the word 'repent' is not the beginning of the gospel, though it has to come early in our own discipleship. The beginning of the gospel is always 'Come and see'. Come and see the glory. Come, look upon the holiness. Come, let yourself be touched by the wonder. Perhaps that is why Luke does begin with angels and annunciations, wondrous births and songs of praise before ever he brings John the Baptist on to the stage with his call to repentance. Certainly it is why his warning of signs of the end in the sun, the moon and the stars – so much part of the Advent message – waits until he has been able to say repeatedly 'Come and see' and told the stories that reveal the holiness and draw us to our knees. For all that Advent begins with pictures of the end, the second coming and the judgement, the Gospel

15

writers first recount the birth, the baptism, the transfiguration, the gracious teaching and the acts of healing and power that reveal the glory in our midst.

If we turn to the fourth Gospel, John the Baptist himself makes his own most compelling appeal when he says, as Jesus draws near, 'See the Lamb of God, who takes away the sins of the world' (John 1.29). The stimulus to repentance is to see the glory of God and to see that glory in the face of Jesus Christ. Repentance comes in response to the revelation of divine glory.

But seeing is not quite enough; or, perhaps more accurately, seeing almost inevitably leads to something else. Baruch speaks of taking off a garment. 'Take off the garment of your sorrow and affliction', he says. There is a kind a stripping bare, a starting again, a standing naked. It is the language of repentance. But then Baruch goes on

> Put on for ever the beauty of the glory from God.
> Put on the robe of righteousness that comes from God.
> (Baruch 5.1, 2)

It is the putting on of a new nature. You can sense the baptismal parallels straight away. Leaving aside the old, putting on the new, we are clothed with Christ. Of course, in the incarnation there is a sense in which there is a laying aside of divinity and the putting on, by Jesus, of the rough garments of humanity, God clothed like John in the camel skin and with a leather belt around him. But the call to us is to lay aside the rough garment of human folly and to begin to wear the beauty of the glory of God. Paul writes to the Corinthians, 'You know the generous act of our Lord Jesus Christ, that though he was rich, yet for your sakes he became poor, so that by his poverty you might become rich' (2 Corinthians 8.9). God put on our rough garments that we might wear the beautiful robe of righteousness. Seeing the glory is important if it brings us to repentance, sets us on our feet and points us in a new direction. However, the invitation is not just to see the glory, but to wear the glory. It is not just about straight paths, but about new clothes.

It is as if Baruch is saying that we need to be shiny figures in a humdrum world: just as in those Christmas scenes in cribs and nativity plays and the like, we need to be like golden haloes and silver wings, shafts of glory in human affairs. It is the Christian vocation to wear the glory, not our own glory (heaven forbid), but to wear the glory of God. 'All flesh shall see the salvation of God' proclaimed John quoting Isaiah, and it turns out that they are to see it because we are to wear it, to wear the beauty, the robe of righteousness and even the diadem of glory.

There is, for most of us, a long way to go. With Eric Milner-White, in his prayer entitled simply 'Advent', we may want to plead:

> O Lord, my years grow long,
> my time short:
> Let me make haste with my repentance
> and bow head and heart:
> Let me not stay one day from amendment,
> lest I stay too long:
> Let me cease without delay
> to love my own mischief,
> and abandon without a backward look
> the unfruitful works of darkness.

But when, in William Temple's words, the self-contentment was first pierced by the shaft of his burning love and we first saw our sins in the light of his holiness and the vision of his purity, something may be stirred. It may be called conversion or repentance or stripping bare. It began, but it is almost certainly not complete. Until it is complete, it brings its tasks and its disciplines.

> Lord, grant me new watchfulness
> to lay hold upon opportunity of good:
> Make me at last put on the whole armour of light:
> Rank me among them who work for their Lord,
> loins girded, lamps burning,
> till the night shall pass
> and the true light shine.
>
> Let me sing the new song,
> following the Lamb whithersoever he goeth,
> loving wheresoever he loveth,
> doing whatsoever he biddeth,
> unto the perfect day
> and for ever and ever.
>
> (Eric Milner-White, *My God, My Glory*)

Already perhaps there has been the putting on of new clothes. They are not the camel skins of John the Baptist. They are the robes that reflect the glory and the holiness of God. They are worn by those who have seen the glory and they will play their part in bringing all flesh to see the salvation of God. They are the armour of light.

The Christian year is not, of course, intended to be pure historical reconstruction. If it were, Advent would concern itself only with John the Baptist's birth and not confuse the issue with the adult John at the Jordan before even we have celebrated the birth of Jesus. As for talk of a second coming, if it came anywhere at all, it would come at the end of the year, not right at the beginning. We do not go through the year pretending we do not know what comes next in the story. There is a treasury of truths and gospel stories and, though we may look at one at a time, we let all the other truths and stories that we have explored over and over again engage with the one we have selected. So in Advent, although at a certain level Jesus has not yet been born, we don't pretend we do not know about the glory we shall see in the crib or what it means to be clothed with Christ or how the power of evil is to be defeated on a cross outside Jerusalem. All those truths and more are present when in Advent we have set before us the vision of God's purity, strip off the old garment of sorrow and sin and begin to celebrate the glory that is in our midst even before Christmas comes round again.

3

Travelling the road of the coming Christ

There is a subtle change of mood towards the end of Advent. The liturgical material changes on 17 December and becomes a kind of countdown to Christmas, and the Gospel reading of each day recounts the stories that precede the birth of Jesus as told in the first chapter of Matthew and then of Luke. We move from a part of Advent that insists that what we are focusing on is the second coming to judge the world at the end of time, to a part where the focus becomes more clearly the baby soon to be born, preparing for Christmas and a first coming that happened long ago.

The reality, of course, as we have already recognized, is that the two comings – the baby of Bethlehem and the king who comes to judge – are strangely merged in all our Advent liturgies. The Advent hymns, though their plain meaning refers to the coming at the end of time, we sing as if they heralded Christmas and the Bethlehem story. There is nothing wrong with that, for we are dealing with mysteries, not of time but of eternity, and this kind of interaction is creative. It helps us unfold the truth. And, in a way, we do not only merge two comings, one past and one future, but introduce a third and more immediate element that almost takes over, a present coming – 'be born in us at Christmas, be born in us today'. We remember with such imagination and longing that we make the past present.

It is St Bernard of Clairvaux in the twelfth century who spells out the threefold coming of the Lord. In a sermon he says:

> The third coming lies between the other two. Two of the comings are clearly visible, but the third is not. In the first coming the Lord was seen on earth, dwelling among us; and as he himself testified, they saw him and hated him. In his final coming 'all flesh shall see the salvation of our God', and 'they will look on him whom they pierced'. The intermediate

coming is hidden, in which only his chosen recognize his presence within themselves and their souls are saved. In his first coming our Lord came in our flesh and in our weakness; in his final coming, he will be seen in glory and majesty. This intermediate coming is like a road on which we travel from his first coming to his last. In the first, Christ was our redemption; in the last, he will appear as our life; in his intermediate coming, he is our comfort and our rest.

(Sermon 5 on Advent, in Robert Atwell, *Celebrating the Seasons*)

It is important not to let this sense of an intermediate present-day coming be seen as simply a Christmas Day experience. The carol may have us sing at Christmas time 'Be born in us today', and there is something very special about Christmas Day itself and supremely about the Midnight Mass of Christmas where we can almost believe ourselves in the stable as Jesus is born. But if being born in us today is simply a heightened religious experience that goes with carols, cribs and bleak midwinter, we have missed the point. And Bernard does not locate it at Christmas. His picture of it as a road that we travel between his first and last coming is helpful, for it suggests a coming that is like a daily feeding of the soul. In fact Bernard does go on to reflect on the need to treasure the word of God and to 'feed on it, digest it, allow its goodness to pass into your body'. 'Do not forget to eat your bread,' he says, 'and your heart will not wither.' Here there is at least a hint that this daily coming and feeding is eucharistic; and, of course, that is part of the truth. A much loved prayer before Communion (one I have used before celebrating the Eucharist for nearly 30 years) begins 'Come, Lord Jesus, in the fullness of your grace and dwell in the hearts of us your servants'. The intermediate and present coming is for many of us focused in the sacramental presence of Christ, which unites us with both his first coming and his final coming. It links us with the child born at Bethlehem, for there Christ dwelt in the body of the baby; and in the Eucharist, however precisely we understand it, he dwells in the bread we receive as his body. It links us with his final coming, for it is a daring anticipation of the feast of heaven, where everyone and everything will have been gathered up into Christ. So the eucharistic coming is certainly part of the picture.

But, just as the intermediate coming must not be restricted to Christmas, nor must it be restricted to the Eucharist. The Eucharist is a meal on the journey, but Bernard's image is of the coming as the journey itself, the road we travel together. Perhaps that is why I respond deeply to a text that Janet Morley includes in *Bread of Tomorrow*. For it speaks of a Christ who comes in such a variety of settings, but all of them clearly in the world of today, not simply relegated to the past or holding out for a future.

Come humbly, Holy Child,
stir in the womb
of our complacency;
shepherd our vision
of the little we need
for abundant living.

Come humbly, Holy Spirit,
to whisper through the leaves
in the garden of our ignorance,
exposing our blindness
to children dying,
hungry and in pain.

Come humbly, Holy Light,
pierce our lack of generosity and love,
scattering our dark fear
of living freely in your way,
poured out in wanton service.

Come humbly, Holy Wisdom,
cry through the empty streets
of our pretence to care,
that the face of the poor
will be lifted up,
for holy is your name.

Come humbly, Holy God,
be born into our rejoicing,
Come quickly, humble God,
and reign.
(In Janet Morley, ed., *Bread of Tomorrow*)

Three comings, past, present and future. But, whichever coming we engage with, the lonely figure who stands on the Jordan bank has something to say to us. 'Repent, for the kingdom of heaven has come near . . . Prepare the way of the Lord, make his paths straight' (Matthew 3.2, 3). This is John's straightforward message, which Jesus himself takes up in his first proclamation when he emerges from the desert. The call to repent and to prepare is the heart of John's message, though he develops it and spells it out in denunciation of hypocrisy and immorality. In the religious sphere, it is the Pharisees who are on the receiving end of his denunciations. In the civil sphere, it is King Herod and his family who are faced with unacceptable truths. John is an uncomfortable figure and his message unpalatable. He confronts us with evil, in ourselves and in our society, and bids us turn around. And repentance is, of course, an appropriate response in all these comings of the Lord.

Repentance was the appropriate response to the coming at Bethlehem. It was appropriate because of the symbolic break in the chain of sin which the scriptures affirm in the virgin birth. It was appropriate because repentance, turning around, starting again and going off in a fresh direction are natural responses to the extraordinary reversal of values that the incarnation implies. For it is a turning on its head of all ideas of status, success and power, and an embracing of new gospel values of humility, vulnerability and love. Even half understanding, how could anyone respond but by repentance? Repent and follow a new path, as fishermen, tax collectors, prostitutes and even rabbis began to do. And it is an appropriate response today when we remember with imagination those events that Christmas calls to mind.

John's call to repentance is also the appropriate response to the Church's insistence in Advent that Christ will come again. The good news without the second coming and the judgement is a selling short of what Jesus came to proclaim. It is a gospel without guts. We shall all have to give an account of our lives. In what direction have we been pointing and trying to go? Has it been the path of waywardness and evil or, challenged and repentant, have our eyes been fixed on Jesus and on salvation through faith in him? John's call to repentance challenges us to turn away from sin whenever we think about our eternal destiny and the consummation of all things at the end of time.

But there is also that prayer that Christ may be born in us today that rightly finds a place in Advent, an intermediate coming. This is when we lay hold on the past so imaginatively that it is drawn into the present and when the future is so focused that it is anticipated now. When we find ourselves saying 'be born in us today' and wanting the coming of Jesus as present reality, once again wild, uncomfortable John has his proclamation, 'Repent, turn away from sin, banish evil.' For that is the way to prepare for him and to make space for him to be born in our hearts.

What does it mean to repent, to turn away from sin and to banish evil? This is a vast area of theological exploration, and we can only begin to look at it here. But here are two important starting points.

The Christian repents, first of all, by recognizing the reality of evil. Although the Bible is strong on the reality of evil and the liturgy is full of it in Advent, it often seems that our contemporary Christian thinking has gone soft on it. We fail to recognize its seriousness in either ourselves or our society. Somehow we need to find the self-perception, the humility and the sorrow to say with Christina Rossetti:

> Wearied of sinning, wearied of repentance,
> Wearied of self, I turn, my God, to thee;
> To thee, my judge, on whose all-righteous sentence
> Hangs mine eternity:
> I turn to thee, I plead thyself with thee, –
> Be pitiful to me.
>
> Wearied I loathe myself, I loathe my sinning,
> My stains, my festering sores, my misery:
> Thou the beginning, thou ere my beginning
> Didst see and didst foresee
> Me miserable, me sinful, ruined me, –
> I plead thyself with thee.
>
> I plead thyself with thee who art my maker,
> Regard thy handiwork that cries to thee;
> I plead myself with thee who wast partaker
> Of mine infirmity,

Love made thee what thou art, the love of me, –
I plead thyself with thee.
                    (*The Works of Christina Rossetti*)

It may well be that we recognize that there are some things seriously wrong in our lives. We know we fall short. At a personal level we may be conscious of our failure and our need both to turn away from sin and to accept God's mercy and forgiveness. But most of us too easily excuse or turn a blind eye to the evil that grips aspects of our world. Advent in general and John the Baptist in particular seem to tell us to stop fooling ourselves. Evil is real. It is all around us. There is good in all around us too, of course, and, if we are richly blessed, we encounter the goodness much more than the evil. But the evil is real and it is to be identified and resisted. If it were not real, there would have been no need of a Saviour born at Bethlehem, banishing the darkness, letting in the light, from the crib to the cross and on to the consummation at the end of time. So, if we are to turn from evil, we must recognize it for what it is.

Second, we need to recognize where evil grows. The sores fester, to use Christina Rossetti's image, in the human soul. Evil does exist in other ways, but evil as a kind of force in nature, loose in the atmosphere, so to speak, is a difficult idea to get hold of, and it is certainly not the principal way in which the Christian faith pictures it. The normal breeding ground of evil is in the hearts, minds, souls and bodies of men and women. It is not just in some particular men and women who have fallen victim or sold themselves to the devil, as people say, but in the hearts, minds, souls and bodies of the whole human race. For all the good and love in our lives and for all our yearning for God, which are real, there is no area of our lives in which sin has no foothold. Even in the best parts of our character – the loving parts, the caring parts – jealousies and selfishnesses creep in.

Therefore, part of how we resist evil on a global level is by meticulously resisting it in ourselves. When we examine our consciences, confess our sins, receive forgiveness and accept the restored relationship with God that comes each time we are penitent, it is not just that we are put right with God, crucial as that is. It is also, to put it graphically, another nail in the devil's coffin. My little bit of penitence, my fresh resolution and my turning to the divine mercy and forgiveness for the things that may seem rather insignificant sins, compared with the evils of the world, are nevertheless part of the combating of evil. They score points on the side of the angels. So we need to be diligent never to neglect the pursuit of personal integrity and holiness. Every human heart in which sin does not fester or keep its foothold is part of the banishment of evil from this earth.

Christmas is a corporate time. People come together, rejoice together, eat together, drink together (though some are left out in the cold). But John the Baptist never seems a very social sort of animal and always seems to be talking to individuals. To each individual: 'Repent, turn away from sin, banish evil.' To each individual: 'Prepare the way of the Lord.' Each individual is invited to call to mind the birth at Bethlehem and let its divine reversal of expectations draw out of them repentance. Each individual is invited to look to the future and the judgement and, lest it come like a thief in the night, to be challenged to repentance. Each individual is invited to be open to every intermediate coming to us who stand between the first coming and the last, and here too to let repentance purify the heart.

Eric Milner-White entitles one of his prayers, 'Three Comings'. For him, the intermediate present-day coming is the second. The third is the final one. He identifies it more with the hour of death than the end of time, but the basic point is the same. The response to all the comings of Christ is love. And love for Christ grows out of self-knowledge, repentance and thankfulness for what Christ has done. It is Jesus, rather than John, who tells us that, for every sinner who repents, there is rejoicing among the angels of God (Luke 15.10).

> Let me love thee, O Christ,
> in thy first coming,
> when thou wast made man, for love of man,
> and for love of me.
>
> Let me love thee, O Christ,
> in thy second coming,
> when with an inconceivable love
> thou standest and knockest at the door,
> and wouldest enter into the souls of men,
> and into mine.

Advent

Plant in my soul, O Christ, thy likeness of love;
that when by death thou callest,
it may be ready,
and burning,
to come unto thee.

(*My God, My Glory*)

4

A God stirs beneath her breast

—————➤•◄—————

The Annunciation to Mary is a feast that Christians celebrate, not at Christmas, but at Easter, and it is more than coincidence that the Church recalls the new beginning of the annunciation as it celebrates the new birth of the resurrection. Nevertheless, as Christmas draws very close, the focus turns from John the Baptist, with his distinctive way of preparing the way for Jesus, to Mary of Nazareth and her part in preparing that way both in her response to the angel and also in everything that flowed from that response.

> Nothing will ease the pain to come
> Though now she sits in ecstasy
> And lets it have its way with her.
> The angel's shadow in the room
> Is lightly lifted as if he
> Had never terrified her there.
>
> The furniture again returns
> To its old simple state. She can
> Take comfort from the things she knows
> Though in her heart new loving burns,
> Something she never gave to man
> Or god before, and this god grows
>
> Most like a man. She wonders how
> To pray at all, what thanks to give
> And whom to give them to. 'Alone
> To all men's eyes I now must go,'
> She thinks 'And by myself must live
> With a strange child that is my own.'

So from her ecstasy she moves
And turns to human things at last
(Announcing angels set aside).
It is a human child she loves
Though a god stirs beneath her breast
And great salvations grip her side.

('The Annunciation', Elizabeth Jennings, *Collected Poems*)

So many poets and artists have tried to catch the mood and tension of that extraordinary encounter and dialogue that Luke presents in the first chapter of his Gospel. Elizabeth Jennings' poem, 'The Annunciation', made a huge impact on me when I first read it more than 30 years ago. It catches something both of the shock and the acceptance of the young woman taken over by God.

In a sense, of course, the Church makes more of Mary than scripture demands. Her role in the story of the world's salvation is crucial. Her 'Yes' to the angel, her acceptance of the divine invitation, is a key element in the story. She is indeed 'full of grace', as the angel affirms in his greeting, but she is full of grace because God invades her, body and soul. You can play up the activity of God and play down the role of Mary, as people have sometimes done, without losing the central truth of the incarnation, the Word becoming flesh. However, more often than not, the Church has not played down her role, but celebrated it and celebrated her, with an almost unlikely extravagance. That is partly, I think, because her story is one of those that illustrates so wonderfully the counter-cultural nature, in almost any culture, of the Christian gospel. We probably lose sight too often of the revolutionary tone of Mary's song, *Magnificat*:

[He] has scattered the proud in their conceit,
Casting down the mighty from their thrones . . .
He has filled the hungry with good things
and sent the rich away empty.

(Luke 1.51–53)

And, hidden within that song also these words:

He has looked with favour on his lowly servant.
From this day all generations will call me blessed.

(Luke 1.48)

Mary's story is counter-cultural because it is about God's favour to the lowly, his exaltation of those without glory, without voice, without power. Mary is the peasant girl who might, like any girl, dream of being a princess, but in reality is destined to marry, not the prince, but the village carpenter. And yet all generations will call her blessed and some will put a crown on her head.

Of course the Church has made more of her than scripture demands for another reason too. She has been the way, through much of Christian history, that the Church can affirm, honour and celebrate the feminine in a religion where God has had a patriarchal, paternal and masculine image. It is an image that Jesus, for all his suffering and the gentleness with which we often portray him, does not fundamentally challenge, for he was a man. Sometimes the picture of Mary has been a male-controlled image of the feminine that has needed correction. In our own day, there are many who have not been content to allow Mary to carry the feminine flag, so to speak, and it has become almost commonplace to want to speak of God as Mother, or even of God as 'she'. For all its dangers, that seems to me to be in certain settings a proper exploration of God's nature and character and is not, of course, entirely new, though spiritual writers of the past, such as Anselm and Julian, have been more interested in Jesus as mother than God as mother.

Yet there is much to be said for a faith that allows God to be Father, Son and Holy Spirit, but celebrates not only the human, but the feminine, in Mary – the one who, though not divine, is crowned with glory and honour. The tradition has always seen the words of Jesus from the cross that the fourth Gospel gives us, where Jesus says to John 'Behold, your mother', as an invitation to the Church to see Mary as a mother for Christians. Certainly in the ancient phrase 'Our Lady' there is the sense that she belongs to us and we to her, in a way that does not undermine, but in fact safeguards, our understanding of God.

But somehow we need to find new ways of thinking and speaking about Mary. For the overall picture we have inherited, with its emphasis on suffering mother, pure virgin and obedient handmaid, presents a kind of feminine submission and passivity that do not do justice to the woman whose collaboration with God changed the world. We need to go back to the annunciation story, so loved of the artists with fair Gabriel and beautiful Mary in dialogue, though the conversation at a deeper level is between the peasant girl and her God. In that dialogue it is revealed that God has a divine purpose. He must come among his people in the person of the Son to be their Saviour. And he has a plan. He will be born as a human baby. He will, as Paul says in his letter to the Galatians, be born of a woman (Galatians 4.4). And how is this to be? Through the collaboration of Mary of Nazareth, whom the angel tells us is 'full of grace' even before the Holy Spirit has come upon her and the power of the Most High overshadowed her. The language of the annunciation, although it is not exactly the language of invitation and acceptance (in the end God is saying what he wants) has about it the sense of a God who is looking for one who will collaborate with him. When Mary says, 'I am the handmaid of the Lord, let it be to me according to your word', we speak traditionally of Mary's response as obedience. But to me her 'Yes' is something much more exciting and life-giving than a kind of resigned obedience. It is the 'Yes' of the willing collaborator, the co-worker. Perhaps a Mary full of grace was bound to say 'Yes', but, in a way, I want to cling to the idea of a God who holds his breath, waiting and hoping that it will be 'Yes' that she says. And he is not disappointed.

So the incarnation comes about through a wonderful partnership of the human and the divine, the Virgin and the Holy Spirit, the initiative God's of course, but the human response vital to the enterprise. Because it was a wonderful and equal (at least in a certain sense) partnership of the human and divine, its fruit was Jesus Christ, truly God and truly a man, utterly and equally human and divine. That is the equality the Nicene Creed is wanting to affirm when it says

> For us and for our salvation he came down from heaven,
> was incarnate from the Holy Spirit and the Virgin Mary
> and was made man.

> (*Common Worship*)

That is the picture of Mary the collaborator with the Creator and it is an insight that is important for the clue it gives to the character of God. If the annunciation is anything to go by, he is the collaborative

God, always on the look-out for partners. He thrives on partnership and does not believe in doing things on his own. He asks you and me to come on board some grand endeavour or some very modest piece of divine initiative and, yes, with a certain vulnerability that our forebears did not recognize, holds his breath and waits for our response.

Of course the most profound of the theological descriptions of Mary, that often turn into titles, is the Greek *theotokos*, the one who carries God. Because that does not translate well, the Western equivalent is *mater dei*, the Mother of God, but, although that is theologically orthodox, it is a slightly uncomfortable phrase, liable to misunderstanding, and almost seems to say too much. So we do better to stay with *theotokos*, god-bearer. Because Mary is full of grace, because of her role as collaborator, the Spirit works in her and she carries in her womb the one who is as much God as he is human, Jesus Christ. Elizabeth Jennings captures the truth of it with great simplicity in the final lines of her poem 'The Annunciation':

> It is a human child she loves
> Though a god stirs beneath her breast
> And great salvations grip her side.
> (*Collected Poems*)

The insight of Mary as *theotokos* is worth holding on to because, at the very heart of faith, she is not the one who matters. She is simply a vessel for the divine, the means by which God came uniquely among a people in a way that has changed everything. Because she was that vessel, all generations are to call her blessed, but she does not point to herself. She carries Christ into the world. That was how he came first among his people, hidden in the Virgin's womb.

As with collaborator, so with god-bearer, Mary is a model for Christians. Christ's glory fills the universe, but he is not seen on earth as he was in the days of his incarnation. His glory fills the universe, but he is hidden among his people; hidden, not in their wombs, but in their hearts and minds and bodies, and wherever they go they carry Christ into the dark, hurting and unexpecting places of the world. In other words, for all the uniqueness of Mary as *theotokos*, every Christian is also called to be a god-bearer. We must, every day in every way, carry Christ into every place and every circumstance where his love and compassion and life are longed for.

St Bernardine of Siena, writing in the fifteenth century, says of Mary that 'the whole Church stands in the debt of the Virgin Mary, since it was through her childbearing that it was able to receive Christ' (Second Sermon on St Joseph: opera S Bernardini, VII, 1627–30, in Robert Atwell, *Celebrating the Saints*). But he goes on to say immediately that, after her, it owes special thanks and honour to Joseph. For the Christmas story does not tell of a Mary who stands for long on her own. Despite Elizabeth Jennings' 'Alone to all men's eyes I now must go', there is Joseph, the 'righteous man' as Matthew calls him. Indeed Matthew, for all that he wants to affirm the virginal conception, gives prominent place to Joseph, 'the son of David'. He too has his visits from the angel. To Joseph also there is an annunciation.

Matthew's concern, of course, is to show the Jewish people for whom he is writing that Jesus born at Bethlehem is indeed, as the prophets foretold, the descendant of David. The opening verses of Matthew's Gospel are an elaborate and fascinating genealogy, 14 generations from Abraham to David, 14 from David to the Babylonian exile, 14 from the exile to the birth of Jesus. So, though the whole thrust of Matthew's account, in which Joseph is reassured and accepts his role as the guardian of Mary and her child, is on the virgin birth, Joseph's role is nevertheless not played down. He too is part of the story.

Bernardine says:

> Joseph was the specially chosen man through whom and under whom Christ entered the world fittingly and appropriately . . . For in him the Old Testament finds its fitting close. In him the noble line of patriarchs and prophets comes to its promised fulfilment. What God in his goodness had offered to them as a promise, Joseph held in his arms. Clearly, Christ cannot now deny to him the same intimacy, respect and high dignity which he gave him on earth, as a son to his father.
>
> (In Robert Atwell, *Celebrating the Saints*)

Scripture tells us little about Joseph. There is the subtle irony of his trade, the village carpenter. Jesus grows up, as we may picture him, familiar with wood and what can be done with it, as if it were preparing him for Calvary and the wood of the cross, where he works wonders with the wood that becomes the sign of universal salvation.

There is the tradition, owing little to scripture, of Joseph as the aged husband of the young Mary. The only sense in which it does relate to scripture is in giving some rationale as to why Jesus has brothers and sisters, for the tradition decides they are the children of a first marriage by Joseph. But this is pure conjecture, though not without theological motive. An aged Joseph also accounts for why he seems no longer to be on the scene later in the story.

For all that we know so little of Joseph, and for all that we are in a world of poetic storytelling of angels and dreams, there are lessons to be learned from him. We can receive and reflect upon the picture of a devout working man ('righteous' as Matthew calls him), with a real sense of family, both that from which he was descended and also that for which he was to care. He was a man with a sense of right and wrong, with no desire to hurt or cause scandal (planning, remember, to dismiss Mary quietly). He had an ear open to God, with a trust and faith to believe what he heard and to act upon it. There are good things there to hold on to when Christmas draws near. A reverence about family, a concern for right and wrong, an openness to God, a trust and a faith to hear and act can all be learned from Joseph. He cannot but help create in those who meditate on his part in the story a proper receptivity to what God is offering in the Child of Bethlehem.

Yet even on the threshold of Christmas, when thoughts naturally turn to Mary and Joseph and, beyond the annunciations, to the journey to Bethlehem, the focus still needs to be on the unborn son of Mary. It is worth staying for a little longer with Matthew, who gives Joseph's story such prominence, and to ask what we learn from him about the baby in Mary's womb.

The genealogy complete, Matthew begins his account 'Now the birth of Jesus the Messiah took place in this way' and, of course, the translation may equally be the 'Messiah', the 'Christ' or the 'Anointed One'. At the end of the chapter he will tell us that, when Mary had borne a son, Joseph named him Jesus. The name means literally 'God is our salvation' and therefore 'God is Saviour'. Between those two names, which is what they have become, Christ and Jesus, we find a third, Emmanuel. That is the title in Isaiah's prophecy, taken up by Matthew in the Gospel: 'Look, the virgin shall conceive and bear a son, and they shall name him Emmanuel' (Matthew 1.23). Matthew has changed Isaiah's 'young woman' (Isaiah 7.14) to 'virgin' to strengthen the sense of the new beginning. He has also given us the translation of Emmanuel. It means, he tells us helpfully, 'God is with us'.

Messiah, Saviour, Emmanuel. What stupendous claims Matthew makes for the baby whose birth he tells in a single verse at the chapter's end. For him, no journey to Bethlehem, no details of census, inn, manger, angels or shepherds, though he will go on to tell of the visitors from the east, but other than the star over the house, no picture of what we would call the Christmas scene. Simply, to relapse into the beautiful reticence of King James' version of the Bible, 'He knew her not until she had brought forth her first-born son: and he called his name Jesus' (Matthew 1.25, AV). Matthew has less interest in the question 'How did it happen?' He has much greater interest in its meaning and in the question 'Who is this?' He is Messiah, he is Saviour, he is Emmanuel, God with us. That is what Matthew wants us to think about. And, if Luke's picture takes over on Christmas Day, with the overcrowded inn, the angels singing, the shepherds wondering, Mary pondering, and probably all sorts of unscriptural details that give the story its charm – whether bleak midwinters, lambs or little donkeys – then before all that, on the threshold of Christmas, we need to engage with Matthew's 'Who is this?' And the ultimate answer is 'The one who shows us God.'

With Mary, the peasant girl some call queen, and Joseph, the son of David, who was righteousness personified, we need to ponder Matthew's question and to meditate on the three answers he seems to be giving. Matthew tells you that the Virgin's son is Messiah, God's anointed one. He is Saviour, God is our salvation. He is Emmanuel, God is with us. For all that Matthew has but one angel to act as herald, where Luke has a multitude of the heavenly host, nothing about Christmas is better news than this – he is Messiah, Saviour and Emmanuel.

5

Sing with me, dance with me

⟡

Christians hardly ever read the first chapter of Luke's Gospel, with its 80 verses, at one sitting or even story by story sequentially over a very few days, though the daily readings for the Eucharist from 19 to 24 December do exactly that. First in that chapter is the annunciation by the angel Gabriel to old Zechariah as he ministers in the temple, with its news that he and Elizabeth are to be parents, and that the child is destined for remarkable things. And then the scene changes. We go with the angel from Jerusalem to the village of Nazareth for a second annunciation, this time to a young woman – not much more than a girl – to Mary. For she too is to have a baby, and this one not just destined for remarkable things. This one is to be the son of God. The chapter will end with the story of the birth of Zechariah's and Elizabeth's child, with his naming, John, and with his father's song of prophecy and praise. And the opening of the following chapter will complete the symmetry when it tells of the birth of Mary's child at Bethlehem.

But between those two annunciations and those two births is the tale that connects one annunciation and birth to the other. Old Elizabeth, too old really for this child-bearing business, is embraced by her young cousin, Mary, almost too young to be a mother, and in that encounter there is excitement, affirmation, joy, sheer delight, and it turns into a song, 'My soul magnifies the Lord.' 'The Visitation of the Blessed Virgin Mary to Elizabeth' the calendar calls it, though 'visitation' is too formal a word for this affectionate meeting. The Church celebrates the event on 31 May, but the story belongs, where Luke puts it, at a pivotal place between annunciations and births and helps to make sense of both.

'In those days Mary set out and went with haste to a Judean town in the hill country' (Luke 1.39). Luke does not tell us why she went, nor why she travelled with haste. It is a simple description. Why mention haste? How are we to imagine Mary's journey, her motive for going, her thoughts as she travels, so soon after the angel has brought the news that is changing her life?

Here is a man's version. The writer is Jeremy Taylor, seventeenth-century Anglican divine.

> Let us notice how light and airy was the coming of the Virgin, as she made haste over the mountains; her very little burden which she bears hindered her not but that she might make haste enough; and as her spirit was full of cheerfulness and alacrity, so even her body was made airy and full of life. And there is this excellency in religion that when we carry Christ within us, his presence is neither so peevish as to disturb our health, nor so sad as to discompose our cheerfulness, but he recreates our body by charity and by securing God's providence over us while we are in pursuit of the heavenly kingdom. For as the Virgin climbed mountains easily, so there is no difficulty in our life so great, but it may be managed by those assistances we receive from the holiest Jesus when we carry him about us.
>
> ('The Life of our Blessed Lord and Saviour Jesus Christ',
> in Charles Eden, ed., *The Works of Bishop Jeremy Taylor*)

Jeremy Taylor pictures a rapturously joyful Mary, apparently without a care in the world, the early months of pregnancy clearly giving her no trouble. She is happiness itself, the journey is easy and the mountains are no obstacle. For all the attraction of this light and airy coming, I suspect Elizabeth Jennings, in her poem 'The Visitation', bringing a woman's and a poet's mind to bear on that journey, has more to teach us.

> She had not held her secret long enough
> To covet it but wished it shared as though
> Telling would tame the terrifying moment
> When she, most calm in her own afternoon,
> Felt the intrepid angel, heard
> His beating wings, his voice across her prayer.
>
> This was the thing she needed to impart,
> The uncalm moment, the strange interruption,
> The angel bringing pain disguised as joy,
> But mixed with this was something she could share

And not abandon, simply how
A child sprang in her like the first of seeds.

And in the stillness of that other day
The afternoon exposed its emptiness,
Shadows adrift from light, the long road turning
In a dry sequence of the sun. And she
No apprehensive figure seemed,
Only a moving silence through the land.

And all her journey was a caressing
Within her mind of secrets to be spoken.
The simple fact of birth soon overshadowed
The shadow of the angel. When she came
Close to her cousin's house she kept
Only the message of her happiness.

And those two women in their quick embrace
Gazed at each other with looks undisturbed
By men or miracles. It was the child
Who laid his shadow on their afternoon
By stirring suddenly, by bringing
Back the broad echoes of those beating wings.

(*Collected Poems*)

They stand there, these two highly pregnant women, and the words of reverence and joy pour out, stories told, secrets shared, enfolded in an intimacy of joy. But it always seems a strongly physical meeting. It could not fail to be, with two women great with child. Luke tells us twice about the baby that leapt in Elizabeth's womb: 'Blessed are you among women, and blessed is the fruit of your womb. And why has this happened to me, that the mother of my Lord comes to me? For as soon as I heard the sound of your greeting, the child in my womb leapt for joy' (Luke 1.42–44). It is a physical, bodily response to the arrival of the mother of the Lord that Elizabeth experiences.

And then comes that lovely song. It seems like an extension of the exclamation with a loud cry that Elizabeth utters when Mary appears. Again it is almost physical. Scripture doesn't quite say it, but I go with Edwin le Grice's paraphrase of the *Magnificat*:

Sing with me a song of gladness,
Dance with me with one accord:
Small I am, but he has called me,
Chosen me to bear his Word.
He is God, my King, my Saviour:
Praise and magnify the Lord.

Call me happy, all God's people,
Sing his praises, everyone:
Me, his servant, poor and lowly,
Chosen mother of his Son,
Channel of his grace and mercy:
See what wonders he has done.

In the joy of our salvation,
For the glorious victory won,
Sing with me to God the Father,
Dance with me to God the Son:
In the love of God the Spirit
Glorify the Three in One.

(*Sing Together*)

There's a physicality; their encounter and their greeting are both of body and of soul.

Body and spirit are often presented as opposites. The religious person is not much concerned with the body, but intent on the things of the spirit. Sometimes law and spirit are contrasted, sometimes flesh and spirit, sometimes body and spirit. But always it is spirit that seems the more religious. And that is fair enough, most of the time, not least because the scriptures often move backwards and forwards between spirit, lower-case 's', my spirit; and Spirit, upper-case 'S', Holy Spirit, the Spirit of God. The Holy Spirit conspires with my spirit, animating my spirit, so that I may be filled with the fullness of God. Spirit wins hands down and body has not got a chance.

Yet the visit of Mary to Elizabeth is a story full of body, and the Christmas story is a physical one of blood and birth and body in the stable. The Letter to the Hebrews has something interesting to say on this. In chapter 10 there is this fascinating sentence:

When Christ came into the world, he said,
'Sacrifices and offerings you have not desired,
but a body you have prepared for me'.
(Hebrews 10.5)

It is fascinating not least because it is a mistranslation of the Old Testament original. 'Sacrifices and offerings you have not desired,' says Psalm 40 in the Hebrew, 'but my ears you have opened.' Somehow in the translation into the Greek, 'my ears you have opened' has become 'a body you have prepared for me'. It may just have been the mistake of a lazy copyist, but it enables the writer to make a profound theological point. God's answer to a system of sacrifice that has failed to achieve the salvation of the human race is not to make us hear better – 'my ears you have opened' – but to prepare a body to receive his eternal Son. Into the body of Mary by the operation of the Holy Spirit comes the Word who takes our flesh. 'A body you have prepared for me.'

Of course this emphasis on the physical, the bodily, is not in antithesis to the spirit. Mary and Elizabeth in their beautiful meeting are filled with the Holy Spirit. It was the Spirit that worked so effectively within Elizabeth that she exclaimed, 'Blessed are you among women and blessed is the fruit of your womb.' It was the Holy Spirit conspiring with her spirit that brought those words to her lips. And Mary herself, in her song, magnifies the Lord, and her spirit, she says, rejoices in God her Saviour. Her spirit and the Spirit of God within her. Within her, of course, in a unique way, for the angel has told her that the power of the Most High will overshadow her, for that which is growing within her is of the Holy Spirit. Here is the body, prepared for the Lord, filled with the Spirit.

Body and spirit together, not opposites, not pulling us in different directions. Paul has something important to say about it in his first letter to the Corinthians: 'Do you not know that your body is a temple of the Holy Spirit within you, which you have from God, and that you are not your own? For you were bought with a price; therefore glorify God in your body' (1 Corinthians 6.19–20).

Our spirits, your spirit and my spirit, co-operate with the Spirit of God, come into a conformity with God's Spirit in a way that is exciting and enlivening, and the setting for that is our body. It is in our body, in our walking and embracing, our loving and touching, our hearing, our seeing and saying that the Spirit of God can be at work in us and through us. That was magnificently true of Mary, but it is of each Christian that Paul wrote 'your body is a temple of the Holy Spirit'.

There is just one more thing that needs to be said about the body. It runs through Mary's song, through this story and through much of the Christmas proclamation. When our bodies are the temples of the Spirit, there is something about the manner in which we use them. It is to do with littleness. The prophet Micah talks about Bethlehem as 'one of the little clans of Judah' (Micah 5.2). He shall be great, the one who is coming, but he will be enabled to come because of what happens in Bethlehem, one of the little clans. In her song, Mary speaks of herself as a lowly servant: 'The Lord has done great things', but it is through the humble one, the little one, that he has lifted up the lowly. Whenever the Spirit comes, it is into the humble person, the lowly little body. It was so when the Spirit descended at Pentecost in wind and flame on those ordinary little men who were to turn the known world upside down. For 'he has lifted up the lowly'.

> Come humbly, Holy God,
> be born into our rejoicing,
> Come quickly, humble God,
> and reign.
> (In Janet Morley, ed., *Bread of Tomorrow*)

However, as well as being physical, this encounter between Mary and Elizabeth is vocal. Mary finds her voice, and out pours the song that has been sung more than any other through 2,000 years of Christian history. Forget for a moment Mary the mother and Mary the virgin. This is the moment of Mary the prophet. The world of the Bible is a man's world and the voice of women is often silenced. There are some exceptions in the Old Testament era – Deborah, Hannah, Judith, Esther – but they are the exceptions. The heroines of the old covenant are a strange group. It is a rewarding exercise to study those extraordinary opening verses of Matthew's Gospel, the list of men who 'begat', all the 42 generations from Abraham to Jesus. There is much about the men, the 'begatters', not much about the women who laboured to bring each new son to birth. But in this fascinating genealogy, just occasionally a woman gets a mention. There is Tamar, involved in incest; Rahab, the prostitute who helped the Israelites to capture Jericho; and Ruth, the outsider who came home with the widowed Naomi. There is Bathsheba, seduced by King David, and there is Mary. It is an extraordinary list of marginalized women, and none of them has a voice until Mary. But then along comes Mary, another marginalized woman, the one found pregnant before she and Joseph had come together, the one to be set aside, divorced, quietly. For all we know, the journey to the hill country to visit Elizabeth may have been to make her invisible at home to reduce the scandal. And suddenly Mary, in an ecstatic dialogue with her cousin Elizabeth – another woman despised and marginalized for her barrenness – finds voice and sings her song, makes the protest and speaks the prophecy for the marginalized, the poor and the downtrodden. And it is a woman's voice. The prophets of old were Isaiah and Jeremiah, Micah and Hosea, Ezekiel and Malachi and more, more men; but now, in that authentic tradition, the spokespeople of the Lord, comes Mary the prophet. It is a woman's voice.

The danger, of course, is that we are so used to this protest song, *Magnificat*, because the Church sings it every evening and has made it safe with pleasing musical melodies, that we do not hear its radical message and its challenge. This is the song of feminine humanity and of downtrodden humanity that has found its voice.

> He has looked with favour on his lowly servant.
> From this day all generations will call me blessed;
> the Almighty has done great things for me . . .
> He has shown strength with his arm
> and has scattered the proud in their conceit,
> casting down the mighty from their thrones
> and lifting up the lowly.
> He has filled the hungry with good things
> and sent the rich away empty.
>
> (Luke 1.48–49, 51–53)

Nevertheless, as Bede wrote in the eighth century:

> It is an excellent and fruitful custom of holy Church that we should sing Mary's hymn at the time of evening prayer. By meditating on the incarnation in this way, our devotion is kindled, and by remembering the

example of the Mother of God, we are encouraged to lead a life of virtue.

(Homily 1, 4; CSSL 122, pp. 25–26; ET by ICEL,
in Robert Atwell, *Celebrating the Saints*)

More than 12 centuries later, both the custom and its appropriateness remain, but perhaps Mary's radical song needs to kindle in its singers not only an encouragement to virtue, but to prophetic word and action. For here stands this young woman, carrying a child, not preoccupied with herself, but utterly engaged with God's justice, his bias for the poor and his judgement on the exploiters. She is the articulate herald of a new order, the one that her Son will bring into being. And in response the Church today needs to be listening out for the contemporary prophets, the people who listen to what God is trying to say to a deaf world and who find a voice to express it. Women and men, young and old, need to see visions, dream dreams and articulate what God is saying to an alienated world, to a damaged Church, and to people for whom even the rumour of God's reality is being lost. We have become comfortable people. We have lost our radical cutting edge. We have ceased to be predominantly among the marginalized and the dispossessed and we have lost the passion to speak for them. But God is for them. His Son lived among them. Mary was their prophet. I cannot hear her song, let alone sing it, without being ready to look for the prophetic message in my own community or even to discover that it is going to be heard only when I find my voice.

So the intimate rapturous meeting of these two women, in whom God is working in an extraordinary way, is not just a simple yet appealing story with a human interest between more significant events that deserve our attention more. This meeting signals important things. It illustrates Paul's teaching that our bodies are temples of the Holy Spirit. It tells us that, in the coming of Christ, women can find their voice. It shows Mary to be the prophet of the new order. It gives us the song of the holy, humble God. In all these ways it heightens our readiness for the birth of Jesus, who will himself embody God, who will affirm women as much as men, will champion the poor and the dispossessed and will reveal, as no one else could do, the holy, humble God.

Above all else it anticipates the joy of the birth of Jesus. 'Joy' is the word that Elizabeth uses. 'As soon as I heard the sound of your greeting, the child in my womb leaped for joy.' And the whole mood of the encounter is of joyful intimacy. And here Jeremy Taylor and Elizabeth Jennings agree. 'It is not easy to imagine what collision of joys was at this blessed meeting', says Taylor. Elizabeth Jennings has:

> When she came
> Close to her cousin's house she kept
> Only the message of her happiness.
> ('The Visitation', *Collected Poems*)

And it is interesting that, whereas scripture tells us that 'Mary said' her *Magnificat*, we always call it her song. There is music in its rhythms, for joy in God's promises always breaks into singing and sometimes into dancing too. Here is sheer joy in the goodness and justice of God, delight in what he is bringing about and trust in his promises. Mary's song of joy, *Magnificat*, will soon give way to the angels' song of joy, *Gloria in excelsis Deo*, but both are set to become the songs of joy of Christians in every century since.

CHRISTMAS

6

Inhabiting both messiness and glory

I always remember the sense of thrill as a child each Christmas seeing in the crib the tiny plaster model or wooden carving of the infant Christ, the *bambino*. As I grew a little older I followed with some awe the procession to the crib at the beginning of the Midnight Mass, the priest carrying that tiny figure and placing it in the manger before he blessed the crib. And later still I carried a candle in that procession. And then, years on, mine were the hands that carried that child and blessed that crib, and mine the knees that knelt before it expressing the worship and adoration of a church full of Christian people on Christmas Eve. That moment has lost none of its mystery, none of its awe. Still the tiny figure, the plaster model, which may be a little gaudy or even a little cheap, symbolizes the miracle at the heart of God's love. For here is the image of a baby, a human child, but here also is a representation of the body of Christ.

'Body of Christ' is a phrase that ought always to be said with reverence. We use it to describe several distinct, but related and similar, mysteries of Christian faith. With whichever meaning we endow it, there ought to be something of the mystery and the awe that we experience on Christmas night. Mary and Joseph look down upon the child in the manger. Any parent looking upon a newborn child cannot but be filled with wonder, as much as with joy, for every human birth is a sign of the creativity, the intricate artistry and the marvellous gentleness at the heart of the universe. But this man and woman look down upon a greater wonder still. For here is God, the one almost always portrayed as strong, powerful, immovable, unapproachable, in the body of a child. The shepherds too, in from the fields, see something new. Quite what they made of it we do not know, but enough to have them praising God for what they had seen.

47

Blessed art thou,
O Christmas Christ,
that thy cradle was so low
that shepherds,
poorest and simplest of earthly folk,
could yet kneel beside it,
and look level-eyed into the face of God.
(From *The Light Shines*, in Janet Morley, ed., *Bread of Tomorrow*)

Shepherds praise. Mary ponders – and so do we. Pondering, reflecting, the Church has come to see that this is no mere aberration in the character of God. It is not a temporary laying aside of his nature, nor a once-for-eternity sojourn in the world of the physical, the material and the mundane. No, this is the ultimate proclamation, the focus at a point in time, of an eternal truth. God comes to us, God may be found by us, touched by us, made real for us, in the tangible world in which we humans live, in a material world, a physical reality. God is in the ordinary, in the mundane, in the unlikely and even in the disappointing. Christianity, of all religions, has grasped the truth that the material and the spiritual are not in opposition. God is so totally involved in our physical world and our tangible experiences that he can find his home and show his true colours, so to speak, in human flesh and blood. He is the sacramental God, for he speaks to us through the material and in so doing sanctifies it. He speaks to us in the body of a child and thus makes holy our human nature. Spiritual gifts and spiritual healing can be communicated not by word only, but by touch, by look, by the warmth of relationship. That's what the *bambino* in the manger says to me. The body of Christ is indeed the clue to the nature of God and the means by which his life is received.

But that theological reflection may seem quite a long way from the simple uncomplicated story that Luke tells. When the moment comes for the baby to be born, Luke, theologian as he may be, expresses it very succinctly: 'She gave birth to her firstborn son and wrapped him in bands of cloth, and laid him in a manger, because there was no place for them in the inn' (Luke 2.7). He does not describe an exhausting and demoralizing trail around Bethlehem looking for accommodation. He does not tell of an innkeeper who comes to the door of the public bar, shakes his head and points to the stable at the back. He does not mention an ox or an ass. He does not explain what it all means. He gives just the barest details: a manger and a birth and no place in the inn. But Christian imagination has made more of the story. In our mind's eye we can all picture the innkeeper shaking his head, but taking pity and leading Joseph and the heavily pregnant Mary and the donkey that has carried her from Nazareth to the place of clean straw and silent beasts where the child is born. And we can give expression to what it all means. This is the moment when God chooses to share our human life, to be one of us, word made flesh, God and sinners reconciled, heaven come down to earth, and earth raised to heaven. And all in a stable because there was no place in the inn.

In a sense the inn of the Christmas story stands for the world of every day, with its ups and downs, joys and sorrows – humdrum, earthy, messy, but some of the time quite a lot of fun. The inn is the place of partying, of friendship, of leisure and of pleasure, of humour, of bawdiness, of showing off and leading on, of seeking attention or finding a corner in which to remain unnoticed. The inn sometimes hides sadnesses, insecurities, searches for identity, seekings for a better quality of loving, a place of forgetting the troubles of today with a toast for a better tomorrow. Pub or bar or inn or club, so it has always been, long before the Key of David or whatever the inn was called where there was no room for Joseph and Mary.

It is from the inn, or maybe the bar or the club, that people come as midnight approaches on Christmas Eve into the churches, often opposite or next door, tinsel sometimes in their hair, just a little inebriated perhaps, but nearly all with real reverence, young people mainly, unchurched every other day of the year, but drawn into the experience of putting the *bambino* into the crib, singing the carols and giving thanks with bread and wine. Out of the pub and into the church. Out of the inn and into the stable.

The stable is the place where Jesus Christ is shown. Not the place where he is known – for he can be known, and is known, in all sorts of settings – but the stable, which on Christmas night is the church, is where he is shown, where we set out to let him be seen.

But why the stable for the Christ to be born? Why the stable for the

Christ to be shown? Surely he should be born in a palace? He comes of David's royal line. He is a prince, albeit a prince of peace. One day he will wear a crown, though one of thorns. He will claim a kingdom and people will call him Lord and Priest and King. Certainly a palace is where the magi from the East will expect to find him. Or should he be born somewhere that will signal something very different? Yes, he should be born in a stable, within earshot of revellers, in sight of animals, at the end of a long journey, with no cot but a manger; the stable but a staging post on a refugee road into exile.

For a stable proclaims that this baby, for all his royal blood, chooses to be one of the poor ones, one of the dispossessed, one of the marginalized. Yes, it is in the stable that Christ should be born and shown.

Another question follows naturally. Where should the news be told? Should it be in the temple? Old Zechariah, with his powers of speech restored now John the Baptist is born, could announce it to the people there as he goes about his priestly duties. Or Simeon and Anna are there just waiting for their moment to tell. After all, this Jesus is the Jewish Christ, their Anointed One, their Messiah. High priests and Pharisees, and even Sadducees, should hear first, surely, for this baby fulfils all that the prophets foretold? He is to be a high priest whose sacrifice will save not only the nation, but the world. Should it be the temple? Or is there a more appropriate place? In the workplace. Not in the temple, the God-place, but in the workplace. Let it be told where ordinary people gather, honest working men about their business, earning their living, trying to make sense of the world they inhabit. Maybe not the revellers in the inn itself, probably too drunk to hear the message. But who is at work at night? Shepherds in the fields, keeping watching over their flocks. Let them hear the message to signify that this baby comes to bring hope and peace to them, more than to high priests and Pharisees. The baby is born poor to be the poor man's friend.

The birth of Jesus is in the stable and the news is told to shepherds at work in the fields because the incarnation is itself the point of meeting, the point of encounter, of God with his people. And the Church invites people in on Christmas Eve because the Church is, or needs to be, an extension of the incarnation, a place of encounter of God with his people.

But first the Church needs to learn that in the birth of Jesus there is a message that it must hear and take to heart before ever it can celebrate the meaning of Christ's coming with the world. What the Church encounters in the incarnation is a God who inhabits the world in all its messiness. He is a God who pitches his tent in a world of refugees, of tyrants, of drunken revellers, of injustices. There was blood in the stable when Mary bore the Christ and there was blood on the ground when she helped lift him down from the cross. And Christian faith affirms that this Christ from birth to death was God. And what a God! He is a God of risks and vulnerability. The kind of Church that such a God must rejoice in is surely a community with ragged edges, misfit members and all sorts of people who would never be able to belong anywhere else. The Church does not always conform to this divine standard. The temptation is to withdraw into the holy huddle of the temple. But 'God so loved the world that he gave his only Son' (John 3.16) and the Son seemed at home in the stable, in the workplace, in the market squares and among the misfits.

Yet the message of Christmas Eve is not just for the Church. There is good news for the society in which it is set. For in the birth of Jesus, with its talk of virgin birth, of angels and of stars, people may encounter a God who, though he does find a home among ordinary people and share their lives, however humdrum, and their relationships, however complex, nevertheless inhabits also another sphere. The sphere of the angels is a sphere of beauty, of holiness, of fragility and of love. He is a God unsullied by ugliness, by profanity, by power and its abuse, by selfishness, hate and greed. He is a God who affirms who we are, sons and daughters, loves us for who are we and yearns for us to be what we could become. He is a God who wants every human being to discover the depth of their being, their true capacity for love, their potential for living to the full. He wants them to be healed, reconciled, whole, alive with every fibre of their body and every longing of their soul, in touch with heaven.

The church opposite the pub on Christmas Eve is charged with enabling that truth to shine through as it did in the stable beside the inn. It may be its only opportunity in the year. For most of the time even people who are conscious that what they seek is healing, reconciliation and wholeness look elsewhere. They are searching for spirituality, but not in the Church. They are even showing interest in angels. Yet even then it is not in the Church that they expect to encounter them. It is not in the Church, except perhaps at Christmas. For just a while at Christmas they may catch sight of the hosts of heaven singing 'Glory to God and peace on earth'. For a moment they may gaze for a while at the little body in the manger, who is the One who can connect them with the God they do not know they seek. In the vulnerable baby, they may catch a glimpse of the divine, an inkling of the truth.

It may be the only opportunity to connect them. It may be the only chance to show that there is a God who inhabits their mundane material world and identifies himself with them in their perplexities, and yet holds out to them also another realm, in which he is equally at home, that can make all the difference to their lives. Somehow in the stillness of the night the church-turned-stable needs to reveal both the messiness and the glory.

It does it, of course, by insisting, in a way that puzzles many who have come, that we need to move on, even on Christmas Eve, from the manger to the altar, or, if you like, from the crib to the cross. The focus is on the body of the baby initially, the *bambino* in the crib. But, for all its appeal, that baby lying there has not quite the power to heal. There's a kind of divine twist, a sort of irony, at which the Christmas story often hints. The road from Bethlehem has always seemed to lead to Calvary. The body of the baby grows, matures and becomes the body of a man. And the man's body is taken and beaten, reviled, scourged, torn and broken. And it is when all the attractiveness of the baby in the manger or the virile beauty of the young man presenting himself on Jordan's bank is disfigured and driven from memory that it becomes the vehicle of God's healing. It is when the body is bleeding, battered and broken that it becomes the sign of salvation. So the heart of the mystery is that, yes, God is in the physical, he is in the material, he is in a body, but it is in the broken body that he redeems.

The people have poured out of the pub and into the church to sing carols, often with an unarticulated understanding that they are being drawn into a deep and divine mystery. It may be tempting to give them only what they know they have come for. But the instinct of the

Church is to take them along as it moves from the manger to the altar, because here is a mystery yet more profound, with greater power to give healing and life in all its fullness.

Move on from the manger to the altar because the miracle of Bethlehem is re-enacted for us in the bread and the wine of the Eucharist. Not only of course at Christmas, but every day the connection is there. Just as every Eucharist is a little Calvary and an Easter meal like the one at the end of the road to Emmaus, so it is also a little Bethlehem.

> Let all mortal flesh keep silence
> And with fear and trembling stand;
> Ponder nothing earthly-minded,
> For with blessing in his hand
> Christ our God to earth descendeth,
> Our full homage to demand.
>
> King of kings, yet born of Mary,
> As of old on earth he stood,
> Lord of lords, in human vesture,
> In the body and the blood;
> He will give to all the faithful
> His own self for heavenly food.
> (Liturgy of St James, paraphrased by
> Gerald Moultrie, *The New English Hymnal*)

We have moved from the manger to the altar, but the talk is still of the body of Christ. The phrase still brings to mind the same sense of wonder and joy. For it is essentially the same mystery of God in the material and the physical, the God whom you can, so to speak, touch. It is the sacramental God, who speaks through the material, and in so doing sanctifies it, and comes to his people in bread and wine, and in so doing gives them the body and blood of Christ. The Christian instinct is to stretch out to receive into hands, as well as hearts, this body of Christ, just as shepherds stretched out hesitant hands to touch the child of Bethlehem, half understanding that here too was God in Christ, God in human body.

So the Midnight Mass is now at the altar. The priest takes the bread, over which he or she has said, 'This is my body given for you.' And what does the priest do with this bread, which in many places will be a beautiful, aesthetically pleasing, perfect rounded host held high? Breaks it. Even on Christmas night the body has to be broken, fragmented, torn. It is that same truth coming through again, the divine twist, the sort of irony. God is in the physical and in the material; yes, God is in a body, but God is in a broken body, for it is in a broken body that he redeems. To be torn apart is the divine destiny of the body of Christ. Even at Christmas that has to be said.

Of course the carollers may not understand very much of that, though we are foolish to underestimate either the power of the liturgy or the imagination of the human heart. But it is good news for those who have left the inn for the stable, and indeed for those still carousing in the inn, among whom also Jesus is hidden, for with them also he is at home. It is good news that God inhabits both the messiness of this world and the glory of another and unites the two when he makes his home in the body of a baby in a manger and stays in that body and lets it be broken to redeem the human race.

> Equality with godhead outpoured overnight!
> How could the Lord and master of us all
> Become so small
> And in this rough deserted place
> Emptied of glory, majesty and might
> Be born the child of Mary, full of grace
> And at her breast
> Find rest?
>
> Leaving his heavenly throne at God's right hand on high
> Clothed in humility, child of the stable,
> How was he able
> To learn obedience, endure our loss,
> Share our humanity, suffer and die,
> That we, rejoicing in his glorious cross
> May evermore acclaim
> His holy name.
>
> ('Kenosis', Edwin le Grice, *Sharp Reflections*)

7

Of the Father's heart begotten

The very attractiveness of Luke's Christmas story and the accessibility of a story of manger, shepherds and angels can lead people to ignore the scriptures that engage more conceptually with the meaning of the incarnation. Indeed, once Christmas Day has been reached and Luke's story told, it is all over for some. Christmas Day is an end, rather than a beginning, and decorations come down well before Twelfth Night, Christmas music ceases in supermarkets and the world is moving on. But for the Christian there is an immensely rich 12 days of Christmas in which to explore the meaning of incarnation.

Of course the heart of many a Christmas service, whether carols or Eucharist, is John's poetic prologue building to its climax in words of profound theological insight: 'And the Word became flesh and lived among us, and we have seen his glory, the glory as of a father's only son, full of grace and truth' (John 1.14). The Christmas Gospel, as it is often called, is there as a kind of verbal icon, with its beautiful, haunting words. But its complex ideas are not often explored. What it wants to teach us is that incarnation is much more than a baby in a manger. Indeed, John has no interest at all in Bethlehem or in angels, shepherds and wise men. He does not wrap his theological truth in a story. In this he is similar to Paul, who likewise shows no knowledge of stories of the birth of Jesus. 'Born of a woman' he says in his Letter to the Galatians (4.4), but there is no hint of a miraculous birth. But, like John, he wants to share with his readers who this Jesus was. He writes to the Colossians:

> He is the image of the invisible God, the firstborn of all creation; for in him all things in heaven and on earth were created, things visible and

invisible, whether thrones or dominions or rulers or powers – all things
have been created through him and for him.

(Colossians 1.15–16)

To enter into the mind of John, and perhaps of Paul, we need to go
back to the opening words of John's prologue: 'In the beginning was
the Word, and the Word was with God, and the Word was God' (John
1.1). We need to remind ourselves that it is of huge significance that
John begins in this way and that it is a conscious reflection of the
beginning of Genesis and of the account of creation. Although it is
too easy to substitute another noun for 'Word', without stopping to
examine the idea of 'Word', let us do so for a moment to get at part
of what this opening is about. 'In the beginning was the Son, and
the Son was with God, and the Son was God.' John is saying that
the one who was born at Bethlehem was there at the beginning, at the
creation. He is echoing a similar kind of passage in Ecclesiasticus,
where the title 'Wisdom' is the equivalent of Word:

> Wisdom praises herself,
> and tells of her glory in the midst of her people.
> In the assembly of the Most High she opens her mouth,
> and in the presence of his hosts she tells of her glory:
> I came forth from the mouth of the Most High,
> and covered the earth like a mist.
> Alone I compassed the vault of heaven
> and traversed the depths of the abyss.

(Ecclesiasticus 24.1–3)

And there is an echo of the same truth when Paul writes in the Letter
to the Ephesians, 'He chose us in Christ before the foundation of the
world' (1.3–4). It is, of course, the truth that the Nicene Creed is
affirming when it says:

> We believe in one Lord, Jesus Christ,
> the only Son of God,
> eternally begotten of the Father,
> God from God, Light from Light,
> true God from true God,
> begotten, not made,
> of one Being with the Father;
> through him all things were made.

(*Common Worship*)

All of these are saying, as John is saying, that the life of the Trinity is not something that comes into being when God decides to have a Son, and the Holy Spirit and the Virgin Mary bring that about. No, the life of the Trinity is part of the way God is, part of the way he has always been. There always has been a Son, a Word, a Wisdom, a Christ, at the heart of God. And that is part of the wonder of Christmas and something to celebrate. The truth, John is telling us, is not that a baby called Jesus was born who would do great things, but that here was the Son, the Word, the Wisdom of God, who had been from the beginning, and now he was a human child.

But the fact that the writers go out of their way to lead us to this truth by reference to creation is highly significant. The fact that John parallels Genesis in his prologue is supremely important for our understanding of the incarnation. For what we are being told is that the incarnation is a new creation, a new beginning. The other Gospel writers are interested in it too, though they express it differently. Luke and Matthew, with their stories of the virgin birth, have the same concern. God begins again, the cycle of human reproduction is interrupted by a divine intervention. There is a new creation and it is God who is bringing it about. Mark, uninterested in virgin births and without the kind of mind that might create a Johannine prologue, nevertheless begins with the Holy Spirit hovering over the waters of the Jordan and descending on the Christ at his baptism in the same way that the Spirit hovered, brooded, over the waters at the creation. In their different ways the evangelists are all pressing home this truth. In Christ, there is a new creation. And Paul, of course, shares that view: 'If anyone is in Christ, there is a new creation: everything old has passed away; see, everything has become new!' (2 Corinthians 5.17).

It does not stop there. For the next truth to unfold in John is that we ourselves are part of that new creation. To be honest, there is an ambivalence in scripture whether the 'we' who are part of this new creation is the Church or the human race. But the crucial thing is that, because of this new creation in Christ at the incarnation, everything has changed. There is a subtle, but lovely, shift in the prologue at verse 14. Until then all has been outside us, so to speak, this breathtaking wondrous revelation, but in verse 14, suddenly he lived among us (yes, among *us*) and we have seen his glory (yes, *we* have seen his glory). *We* have been given power to become children of God. *We* are being caught up in this new creation. At Christmas it is not that the eternal Son comes among us, standing apart from the creation and the sinful world. If he is a light in the darkness, he is not that sort, wrapped up in protective holiness lest he catch something nasty from the world. He is Word become flesh and it is total identification, total infusion, total transformation. It is not the Son who is changed by taking our flesh. It is the human race that is changed as he assumes our nature.

In the fourth century Gregory of Nazianzus spoke about this in one of his 'Orations for Christmas':

> Once more the darkness is dispersed; once more the light is created. Let the people that sat in the darkness of ignorance now look upon the light of knowledge. The things of old have passed away; behold, all things are made new . . .
>
> Light from Light, the Word of the Father comes to his own image in the human race. For the sake of my flesh he takes flesh; for the sake of my soul he is united to a rational soul, purifying like by like. In every way he becomes human, except for sin. O strange conjunction! The self-existent comes into being; the uncreated is created . . .
>
> (Oration 38 'For Christmas', in Robert Atwell, *Celebrating the Seasons*)

For John, redemption is not something that waits until the cross, even less for the empty tomb. For John, incarnation is redemption. Sinful human nature is transformed because Christ has filled it with the divine. 'Hail, redemption's happy dawn' is a Christmas picture, not an Easter one only.

> Songs of praise the angels sang,
> Heaven with alleluias rang,
> When creation was begun,
> When God spake and it was done.
>
> Songs of praise awoke the morn
> When the Prince of Peace was born;
> Songs of praise arose when he
> Captive led captivity.
> (James Montgomery, *The New English Hymnal*)

The angels greeted the first morning of creation. They are back over the fields outside Bethlehem to greet the first morning of the new creation, redemption's happy dawn, when the eternal Son came into the world, filled it and changed it. 'From his fullness we have all received, grace upon grace', as John puts it (John 1.16). Genesis pictures Adam and celebrates the glory of a human being not yet fallen. Now, through this filling up of creation with grace in the incarnation, we have the glory of a human being again, the glory as of the only begotten of the Father, but running over, grace upon grace, into the life of the whole human race.

For Paul also the Church is caught up in the glory. He writes to the Ephesians:

> Blessed be the God and Father of our Lord Jesus Christ, who has blessed us in Christ with every spiritual blessing in the heavenly places, just as he chose us in Christ before the foundation of the world to be holy and blameless before him in love. He destined us for adoption as his children through Jesus Christ, according to the good pleasure of his will, to the praise of his glorious grace that he freely bestowed on us in the Beloved. In him we have redemption.

> (Ephesians 1.3–7)

There is that word again – redemption. Creation is redeemed, restored and renewed. Later, in similar vein, 'you also . . . were marked with the seal of the promised Holy Spirit; this is the pledge of our inheritance towards redemption as God's own people, to the praise of his glory' (1.13–14).

There is a further truth hidden in this passage of Paul's. It lies in those two little words 'in love' in verse 4: 'He chose us in Christ before the foundation of the world to be holy and blameless before him in love.' That brings us straight back to John and the conclusion of his prologue, four verses on from where the Christmas Gospel usually ends, where, in verse 18, he writes:

> No one has ever seen God.
> It is God the only Son,
> who is close to the Father's heart,
> who has made him known.

'Close to the Father's heart' or, in an older translation, 'in the bosom of the Father', it is the inspiration for Prudentius's great fourth-century Christmas hymn:

> Of the Father's heart begotten,
> Ere the world from chaos rose,
> He is Alpha: from that Fountain
> All that is and hath been flows;
> He is Omega, of all things
> Yet to come the mystic Close,
> Evermore and evermore.
>
> By his word was all created;
> He commanded and 'twas done;
> Earth and sky and boundless ocean,
> Universe of three in one,
> All that sees the moon's soft radiance,
> All that breathes beneath the sun,
> Evermore and evermore.
> (Prudentius, *The New English Hymnal*)

Scripture and hymn both affirm that it was love that brought the world into being. It is love, as people say, that 'makes the world go round'. But this is not some sentimental sort of loving that phrases like that suggest. It is the awesome love of the triune God. And, like redemption, it does not wait for Calvary to reveal itself, though the revelation of it there in pain and faithfulness is unsurpassed. No, we meet love first in creation. John's Gospel reveals a truth that Genesis does not quite declare. Here is one of those eternal truths that only in Christ are made visible. It is the truth that there is love at the heart of God, the trinitarian impulse to loving, and it is that that made the world and sustains it in being. It is that love of the Father, and the Son and the Holy Spirit which, Paul tells us in Ephesians, we were chosen to share before the foundation of the world.

So for 12 days of Christmas keep up the decorations and maintain the festive air, for though shepherds and angels may have withdrawn and wise men are yet on their way, there are exciting truths to contemplate and celebrate still. In the birth of Jesus Christ there is redemption, new creation. The fields outside Bethlehem are a new Eden. Gregory of Nazianzus encourages us to 'honour this tiny

Bethlehem which restores us to paradise'. He calls what has come about a miracle, not so much of creation, as of re-creation. We are part of that re-creation, for the glory of God and the glory of Christ has become the glory of humankind redeemed and we are children of God by adoption and grace. Most wonderful of all, we are partakers in the divine loving, close to the Father's heart, where the relationships of the Holy Trinity uphold and sustain the world in being, and all for love.

EPIPHANY

8

Revealing the good news of God

Epiphany is both a season and a day. The 12 days of Christmas complete, we come to the Feast of the Epiphany. The day itself has a complex history. It is Christmas for the churches of the East. In the West, which took it over, it became a second incarnation feast, at first associated with more than one manifestation of the nature and glory of Jesus Christ. In time the celebration of the festival was narrowed down to the coming of the strangers from the East to the young Jesus, as Matthew tells us in his Gospel. The season that follows it is sometimes seen as running until 17 days before Lent (the Sunday called Septuagesima) and sometimes seen as lasting till 2 February, Candlemas. It can either be a season that runs out of steam because, once the magi have come and gone, there seems little left to celebrate, or it is a time that rescues and remembers the other stories that, deep in the tradition, are part of what Epiphany explores.

This broader picture of Epiphany is well expressed in the ancient hymn by the fifth-century Caelius Sedulius. It is found in a number of hymn books, though perhaps not often sung, for a Church that has narrowed Epiphany down to one story will see the introduction of other stories as a confusion.

> Lo, sages from the East are gone
> To where the star hath newly shone:
> Led on by light to Light they press,
> And by their gifts their God confess.
>
> The Lamb of God is manifest
> Again in Jordan's water blest,
> And he who sin had never known
> By washing hath our sins undone.

Yet he that ruleth everything
Can change the nature of the spring,
And gives at Cana this for sign –
The water reddens into wine.
(Trans. Percy Dearmer, in *The New English Hymnal*)

By this understanding of Epiphany there are three key stories or, as an old text puts it, 'three wonders mark this holy day'. They are the coming of the magi, the baptism of the Lord and the sign that Jesus did at the wedding at Cana. And they are not three unconnected events that happen to be celebrated at this point in the year. They are very clearly all 'epiphanies' and there is an important and unitive truth running through them, one that links them with both Christmas, from which Epiphany emerges, and Candlemas, to which it leads.

Mark tells us that, after the baptism of Jesus and the temptations in the wilderness, 'Jesus came to Galilee, proclaiming the good news of God' (Mark 1.14). The coming of Jesus and, through his coming, the proclamation of the good news of God, is what the Church celebrates through the 40 days of the incarnation from Christmas to Candlemas, the Presentation of Christ in the Temple.

The story began long before Christmas Day, with patriarchs and prophets, Baptist and Virgin, each in their own manner preparing the way. But the celebrations began with Christmas Day, and with a newborn baby. They began with a child a day old. It is good to think hard to picture that, for in art the newborn baby is seldom well represented. Either he is precociously advanced, a good deal more than a day old, or else he is just a halo in the straw. But think of a child a day old. Nearly everyone has seen that. The newborn child is so very small, helpless and vulnerable. It is that sight that Mary and Joseph saw, and later shepherds in from the fields. They saw helplessness and vulnerability. But if, like Mary, they knew who this child was, that he was, as the hymn says, 'of the Father's heart begotten', then in the helplessness and the vulnerability they also saw a rare humility. And if, like Joseph, they reflected on the circumstances of his birth – the census from an occupying power, the homelessness because there was no room, the stable setting that had none of the attractiveness we give it – there was at least a hint of suffering.

At an important level, that is what Christmas celebrates. It shows us a newborn child, helpless and vulnerable, teaching us about a strange divine sort of humility, and all with a hint of suffering. It was this that angels proclaimed, a multitude of the heavenly host, hovering over this God-child one day old. It was this that the shepherds saw, going to Bethlehem to see what was come to pass – Mary and Joseph, and the child lying in the manger a few hours old. They did not see a halo in the straw. They knelt to the holy, vulnerable little one, and then returned glorifying and praising, proclaiming what they had seen of the good news of God.

And so to the Epiphany with its wise men from the East. Who knows how far they came, the wise men, astrologers or kings, and how long they took to come? A week or so? A year? Two years even? We do not know. But our instinct when we depict them is to bring them, however unlikely historically, to a holy family still in the stable, still among the beasts, the same angels hovering overhead. We bring them to see the same sight. We bring them to the vulnerable baby who shows us the humility of God. Wise men as they were, perhaps they themselves reflected on this coming of the world's powerful ones to the powerless one. Wise men as they were, they were surely puzzled at least by the foreboding hint of future suffering in the air. There was cruel Herod's determination to rid himself of a rival, his death threat to other helpless children and rumours, which perhaps they heard, of a massacre of innocents. Certainly there was the sense of something ominous that has T. S. Eliot's wise man say:

> Were we led all that way for
> Birth or Death? There was a Birth, certainly,
> We had evidence and no doubt. I had seen birth and death,
> But had thought they were different; this Birth was
> Hard and bitter agony for us, like Death, our death.
>
> ('The Journey of the Magi', in *Collected Poems*)

And then there were their gifts, which have fascinated scholars and poets ever since. The conventional explanation is of gold for a king, incense for a priest, or sometimes for a god, and myrrh for one who is to die. There is an attractiveness in the poem by the seventeenth-century priest Nathaniel Wanley:

The off'rings of the Eastern kings of old
Unto our Lord were incense, myrrh and gold;
Incense because a God; gold as a king;
And myrrh as to a dying man they bring.
Instead of incense (Blessed Lord) if we
Can send a sigh or fervent prayer to thee,
Instead of myrrh if we can but provide
Tears that from penitential eyes do slide,
And though we have no gold, if for our part
We can present thee with a broken heart
Thou wilt accept: and say those Eastern kings
Did not present thee with more precious things.
(Coughlan et al. (eds), *A Christian's Prayer Book*)

Like others before him, Wanley identifies myrrh as a gift 'as to a dying man they bring'. It is a prophetic gift, looking to the day when a woman would anoint the feet of Jesus in anticipation of his burial, and other women would take the spices they had prepared early one morning to anoint the body laid in the tomb. But the other gifts have hints of something similar. If gold is for a king, we know what kind of king this baby was to become. He would be the king whose kingdom was not of this world, the king who would avoid every crown except the crown of thorns. He would be the one whose kingship would be proclaimed only on an inscription on a cross on which he hung. Gold for a suffering king. And incense? Perhaps for a God, and if so for a very different sort of God, but incense also for a priest. Here again this will be a new kind of priesthood, not one where the priest offers the same sacrifices for himself and for the people over and over again, but one who will be both priest and victim, offering himself once for all for the sins of the world. The three gifts all point in the same direction – to the one who will reinterpret kingship, priesthood and divinity through the path of suffering he will tread.

The wise men come to Christ. The adult world kneels to the infant. The men of power bow down to the powerless. The kings discern a strange and divine humility. Suffering is in the air, and life and death seem oddly mixed. If the Epiphany is the revelation of Christ to the nations, what is revealed, and this time to the nations of the earth, is helplessness and vulnerability, with a strange divine sort of humility, and all with more than a hint of suffering.

But Epiphany, we have already noted, is more than wise men. There are three wonders – magi, baptism and water into wine. In the last two of these, we do seem to begin to leave behind the newborn baby. And, at a certain level we do need to leave him behind. Ann Lewin expresses that in her poem, 'Incarnation':

> He's grown, that Baby.
>
> Not that most people have noticed.
> He still looks the same,
> Lying there in the straw, with
> Animals and shepherds looking on.
> He's safe there, locked in that moment
> Where time met eternity.
>
> Reality of course is different,
> He grew up, astonished people with his
> Insight, disturbed them with
> Ideas that stretched them into
> New maturity.
>
> Some found him
> Much too difficult to cope with,
> Nailed him down to fit their
> Narrow minds.
>
> We are more subtle,
> Keep him helpless,
> Refuse to let him be the Man he is,
> Adore him as the Christmas Baby,
> Eternally unable to grow up
> Until we set him free.
>
> By all means let us pause there
> At the stable, and
> Marvel at the miracle of birth.
> But we'll never get to know
> God with us, until we learn
> To find him at the Inn,
> A fellow guest who shares the joy and sorrow,
> The Host who is the life we celebrate.
>
> He's grown, that Baby.
> (*Watching for the Kingfisher*)

In the baptism of the Lord, he is grown to maturity, the young man now, no longer a child, striding towards the Jordan and the baptism of John. He is no longer a baby, but able now to hear and to understand the words of the Father, 'This is my Son, the Beloved, with whom I am well pleased.' No longer a baby, he is able now to sense the descent of the Spirit like a dove alighting upon him. But even in the young man, there is still that strange sort of humility, for he had no need of what John could give, yet he would do what God required and submit to baptism. 'Let it be so now; for it is proper for us in this way to fulfil all righteousness', he says in Matthew's description of the event (Matthew 3.15). Still there is also that hint of suffering, at least if we take into account the fourth Gospel's treatment of this scene at the Jordan. For there at the water the Baptist says, 'Here is the Lamb of God who takes away the sin of the world!' (John 1.29). What a strange acclamation this is, with its implication that this young man will be a sacrificial lamb to take away sin. Furthermore, in the voice from heaven and the descent of the dove there is an overwhelming experience for Jesus that drives him away to take shelter in the wilderness and to be tempted by Satan. Maybe he is now the young man in adult life, but he is vulnerable still.

It is as if we superimpose the image of the young man at the Jordan on the picture of the baby in the manger, and make connections. And indeed that is exactly what the Epiphany season does for us. We sing of the baby, and his visitors from the East, and we gaze still into the crib, at least in our mind's eye, but we celebrate and proclaim that the truths we found in the manger we find over and over again as Christ's glory unfolds. All the stories the Church weaves together and superimposes in this season help us to proclaim this gospel of the incarnation that Jesus came, proclaiming the good news of God.

And to whom does he go with his good news? He goes to those who will reveal that his kingdom is for the helpless, the vulnerable, the humble, and for those who will suffer. He goes to the fishermen – to Andrew and Simon and James and John – and makes them part of his proclamation. These are the fishermen who misunderstand, who fail, who deny, who run away, who weep, or who, if very brave, stand at the foot of the cross. Jesus comes into Galilee and proclaims the good news of God as his teaching and his ministry begin, and still it is a gospel about helplessness, about vulnerability, about a strange sort of divine humility, and with very much more than a hint of suffering. We have moved from shepherds in from the fields to fishermen by the lake, but what they are being shown of the good news of God is very much the same.

The world wants to pack up Christmas and put it away all too soon, and in a sense the world may be right that we have to move on from the baby, but not from the lessons we have to learn about the One who came with all his glory into our midst at Bethlehem. Epiphany gives us the opportunity to assimilate these lessons one by one and see the relationship between them. It enables us to reflect on this great mystery of the birth of the powerless One, who shows us the Father, and to learn how to reveal his glory, or at least to allow him to reveal his glory through us. We hold before us these pictures of the growing boy and then the young man, each revealing glory, but we try not to lose sight of that first scene at Bethlehem, which can illuminate all that follows.

We can do that for the 40 days from Christmas until Candlemas, the Presentation of Christ in the Temple. And here is one of those lovely bits of subtlety in the Christian year. We are led on through Epiphany, apparently letting the baby fade into the background as the young man takes his place, the Spirit comes down, the disciples are chosen, the miracles begin – and then right at the end we are brought back to the baby. We are brought back to the vulnerability and the powerlessness, lest we forget. And here the powerlessness is not just in the baby, in the very young. It is also in old Simeon, with *Nunc Dimittis* on his lips, and ancient Anna, the widow prophetess, fit for nothing but wandering about the temple with a yearning for a Saviour. And here once again we encounter that strange divine sort of humility as the God-child submits to the customs of the Jewish law. Here too is the suffering, as Simeon talks of the fall and the rise of many, the rejection that is to come, and the sword that will pierce the soul of Mary.

Candlemas, the Presentation of Christ in the Temple, is a day of profound significance, a kind of pivot in the Christian year, when all these other stories, like parts of a jigsaw, fit into place, the mysterious connection between birth and death that the wise men perceived finally makes sense, and the Church begins to turn from the incarnation to the passion.

The truth that clarifies is this. Simeon makes it explicit, though shepherds and kings and disciples must have begun to see it and half proclaimed it, and Mary, pondering, must have got there first. The incarnation is about the helplessness, powerlessness, vulnerability, humility, the suffering even, of God himself. The incarnation is not an aberration, a temporary laying aside of omnipotence. It is the way God is. It is the self-constraint in which he has wrapped himself, so that his shaping of our world comes not from interventionist power, but from self-effacing yet passionate love.

That is the truth that reveals itself through Epiphany as the stories are told. It is a revelation that turns out to be, mysteriously and paradoxically, both light and glory. Simeon sings it in his *Nunc Dimittis*: 'A light to lighten the nations and the glory of Israel.' The glory of God in the incarnation is not in his omnipotence, but in his helplessness. The light for the world is in the coming of the vulnerable One.

On the second day of Christmas 2004 the world witnessed an extreme example of one of those acts of nature that inevitably cause people to question the kind of God in which they believe. Nearly 300,000 around the Indian Ocean died in a few moments through the savagery of an earthquake and a tidal wave. Natural disasters are part of our world, but that one was on such a scale that the question about what kind of God we believe in was for many a more insistent one.

'Where was God in the tsunami?' people were asking. There is, of course, no easy answer. I do believe God is the almighty Creator who made the world, this magnificent but volatile planet with its earthquakes and its floods. Part of me, like many before me, even in the scriptures, wants to rail against a God whose creation can wreak such havoc and cause such misery. But I also believe in the helpless, powerless, vulnerable, humble, suffering God, whom Christmas and Epiphany and Candlemas celebrate. And, though there have to be other, more complex answers as well, I believe we need to say in response to the question, 'Where was God in the tsunami?', that he was and is in the helpless, the powerless, the vulnerable, the humble and the suffering, who were overwhelmed by the flood.

There are other truths to be learned through the Epiphany season. There are lessons to be drawn out of the baptism of Jesus, the wedding at Cana and the calling of disciples; and the Presentation in the Temple has other truths to impart. But this good news of the character of the self-emptying God runs through the whole season and is part of the message of each successive story.

9

Manifest in water blest

———⊷◦⊶———

> The Lamb of God is manifest
> Again in Jordan's water blest,
> And he who sin had never known,
> By washing hath our sins undone.
> (Caelius Sedulius, trans. Percy Dearmer,
> in *The New English Hymnal*)

Our forebears were clear that the baptism of Jesus was one of the great epiphanies. Its celebration belonged with the commemoration of the visit of the magi. 'Today Jesus is revealed as the Christ in the waters of baptism', they said. Recognizing that 6 January has been so exclusively taken over by the wise men from the East, the Church now has a distinct feast to mark the Lord's baptism on the Sunday that follows the Feast of the Epiphany itself. Just days after the scene with the magi kneeling and paying homage to the child and opening their gifts, the focus moves to the young man on the Jordan. He appears among the crowd where John is baptizing, submits to baptism, hears a voice from God who calls him his Son, receives the Holy Spirit who swoops down like a dove, and flees to the wilderness.

There is a sense of new creation about this moment. We are in a world of water, reminiscent of Genesis 1, where the earth was a formless void and darkness covered the face of the deep, while a wind from God swept over the face of the waters, the wind that is identified with the Spirit. And here we are again at the water in the baptism of Jesus, and a dove, again identified with the Spirit, broods over the water and then descends upon the One who is designated Son. Or another water story may come into mind. When the great flood is subsiding in Genesis 8, Noah sends out a dove over the waters three times as a renewed earth emerges and a fresh start is held out for humankind.

Then Noah sent out the dove from him, to see if the waters had subsided from the face of the ground; but the dove found no place to set its foot, and it returned to him to the ark, for the waters were still on the face of the whole earth. So he put out his hand and took it and brought it back into the ark with him. He waited another seven days, and again he sent out the dove from the ark; and the dove came back to him in the evening, and there in its beak was a freshly plucked olive leaf; so Noah knew that the waters had subsided from the earth. Then he waited another seven days, and sent out the dove; and it did not return to him any more. (Genesis 8.8–12)

The water of the flood was the drowning place of sinful humanity. But now it almost seems as if the water of the Jordan is sanctified by the baptism of Jesus within it and becomes a sign, not of drowning men, but of sinners cleansed and forgiven. Peter Chrysologos of Ravenna puts it like this:

Today the Holy Spirit hovers over the waters in the likeness of a dove. A dove announced to Noah that the flood had disappeared from the earth; so now a dove is to reveal that the world's shipwreck is at an end for ever. The sign is no longer an olive-shoot of the old stock: instead the Spirit pours out on Christ's head the full richness of a new anointing by the Father. (*Sermon* 160, *PL* 52; ET by ICEL, in Robert Atwell, *Celebrating the Seasons*)

The event is clearly highly significant theologically. It has been neglected through much of Christian history, with so much emphasis on the birth of Jesus that his baptism has been thought to add very little that is new. The account of the baptism does not, for instance, feature in the eucharistic lectionary of the Book of Common Prayer, nor is it mentioned in the creeds. A single line preserves an interest in the Litany of the Book of Common Prayer: 'By the mystery of thy holy Incarnation; by thy holy Nativity and Circumcision; by thy Baptism, Fasting, and Temptation, Good Lord, deliver us.'

Part of its theological significance lies in what it contributed to Jesus's self-understanding. It seems that it was an overwhelming experience that drove him into the wilderness to wrestle with his vocation. Our difficulty is that we are not admitted to the working of his mind. We can only surmise his thoughts as he takes the road to the desert. We cannot even do that, for his journey to the Jordan, for the expectations with which he came, will have depended so much on what has gone before.

And here the evangelists give us such different pictures. In terms of the Church's calendar it may be that we move in one jump from a miraculous birth and the coming of mysterious visitors from the East to the scene at the Jordan nearly 30 years on. But how has Jesus come to the Jordan, and what has prepared him for it? The evangelists tell it differently. We cannot know which of them comes nearest the historical truth, but we can reflect profitably on their different approaches.

We can look first at the approach of the earliest Gospel writer, Mark. For him, the baptism of Jesus is crucial. It is the first story that he tells. John the Baptist appears, and immediately after that Jesus himself. We have to remember that Mark tells no stories of the birth of Jesus, no Mary, no Bethlehem, no Egypt, no interest in childhood. Only Nazareth, but without any detail. He has either never heard the stories or does not see that they are important. For him, it is the baptism that provides the key. Jesus appears from nowhere, as it were, and in the water of baptism receives his call, and is there and then proclaimed the Son of God, the Beloved. And immediately, without further delay, we are into the wilderness experience and the three years of ministry that follow it.

We need to think about a Jesus like that, coming to his baptism from nowhere, perhaps without preparation, perhaps without fore-knowledge, perhaps without nurturing through childhood and beyond along the path of religious awareness. Whether it was like that with Jesus or not (and if Luke is right it was not), it is a variety of Christian discipleship, with which we are familiar and which the Gospels honour. It is the sort of Christian discipleship that does not grow out of upbringing, family or long Christian experience. Like the experience of the apostle Paul on the Damascus road, it comes without warning, almost as a reversal of everything that has gone before, with a freshness, a vigour and often an articulation that longer established Christians find it difficult to emulate.

This is the experience of the people whose faith comes in adult life, apparently out of nothing, though inevitably there have been seeds sown years back, and sometimes one of them has been the grace of

Christian baptism in infancy. The Jesus of Mark's Gospel, the Jesus who comes from nowhere to be anointed as the Messiah, affirms this path to discipleship.

But next consider the picture as Matthew or Luke portray it. The details of the baptism of Jesus are not very different, though both, in their different ways, are keen to show that Jesus did not need to be baptized by John. The detail may not be very different, but the context alters the significance a great deal. For, whereas in Mark the baptism is the first story and we know nothing of Jesus until he appears at the Jordan, in Matthew and Luke the baptism follows on a series of stories from the annunciation, through the birth narratives, to stories about the young child, whether presented in the temple or living a refugee life in Egypt.

Luke alone tells the remarkable story of Jesus, left behind in the temple at the age of 12, found sitting about the doctors of the law, listening to them and asking them questions. They are amazed at his understanding and Jesus responds to his distraught mother, 'Did you not know that I must be in my Father's house?' (Luke 2.41–51). Here is a child acutely aware of his vocation, and it was apparent to all that day by day and year by year he increased, not only in wisdom, but in divine and human favour. He was no ordinary child.

This Jesus, portrayed by Luke and to some extent by Matthew, comes for baptism prepared, nurtured in the faith, with a maturity learnt through 30 years of growing in the things of God. Within such a context, the baptism of Jesus is not a kind of reversal, a fresh start or a new direction: it is a confirmation, an adult recommitment to a whole ethos of trust in God and religious practice in which he has grown up. And whether it was really just like that for Jesus or not (and if Luke was right it was), there is another pattern of Christian discipleship, as real and valid as the other.

Look at it more closely. It is the pattern that justifies the huge resources that the Church puts into education and the nurturing of the young. It is the pattern that places much emphasis on the Christian home, in which are taught the habit of prayer, the discipline of Bible reading, the regular participation in the worship of the Church. It is the pattern that recognizes that those who are drawn into the Church from birth and nurtured within it may grow to Christian maturity and adult commitment from that beginning, rather than coming in, from nowhere as it seems, in later life.

Both paths into discipleship are God-given, genuine ways to salvation. In the early years of Christianity, the vast majority came to faith the Markan way, in adult life, from nowhere. In later centuries, through most of Christian history, though there have always been those whose conversion to Christ has been sudden, an upheaval of all that has gone before, for most the Lucan way of growing from birth to maturity within the Church's orbit has been the way to salvation. In our twenty-first-century society, where many established patterns have collapsed, that is changing. The Markan way may again become the norm.

But what of John, the fourth evangelist? John, like Matthew and Luke, does not plunge straight in with the story of Jesus at the Jordan, though in his case it is that great outpouring of poetry and doctrine in his prologue that precedes the arrival of Jesus at the Jordan. The key difference, of course, in John's account is that Jesus is not baptized at all.

> The next day John the Baptist saw Jesus coming towards him and declared, 'Here is the Lamb of God who takes away the sin of the world! This is he of whom I said, 'After me comes a man who ranks ahead of me because he was before me.' I myself did not know him; but I came baptizing with water for this reason, that he might be revealed to Israel.' And John testified, 'I saw the Spirit descending from heaven like a dove, and it remained on him. I myself did not know him, but the one who sent me to baptize with water said to me, "He on whom you see the Spirit descend and remain is the one who baptizes with the Holy Spirit." And I myself have seen and have testified that this is the Son of God.'
>
> (John 1.29–34)

In John's understanding, which is different from the others, Jesus, the sinless one, has no need of the waters that cleanse. In John's account, Jesus does nothing at all, except let it happen. It is God who acts. It is God who shows John the Baptist the Spirit descending on Jesus. It is God who enables John the Baptist to proclaim that Jesus is the Lamb of God and the Son of God. Jesus is simply recipient.

There also is a lesson to be learnt. Whatever our path to Christian discipleship, whether it be through the long nurturing of the Church or through sudden conversion, it is never what we do: it is always through what God does. We are always recipients, recipients of grace, God's life-giving gift, freely given, generously outpoured. In baptism itself, whether in infancy or in adult life, it is what God does, not what we do. It is his grace that is the key.

Whichever of the Gospel accounts is most accurate, and whatever exactly happened, it was clearly significant for Jesus's self-understanding and vocation. It marked the first very public statement of his unique status. It also changed baptism. The fourth Gospel has John the Baptist tell us that 'the one on whom you see the Spirit descend and remain is the one who baptizes with the Holy Spirit'. And, although the baptism by John was different, Jesus, by his baptism in the Jordan, was seen to be inaugurating something new.

'And now we give you thanks because you celebrated your new gift of Baptism by signs and wonders at the Jordan' prays one of the Epiphany eucharistic prefaces (Proper Preface, based on the Roman Missal, in *The Promise of His Glory*). Any celebration of the baptism of Jesus celebrates also baptism as part of the Christian life. This is part of what the early writers meant when they talked of Jesus 'sanctifying' the waters by his baptism. The baptismal water became a means of grace. But, of course, it is not only the baptism of Jesus that has been played down in Christian theology through the centuries. Through many centuries in many churches, the baptism of Christians has also been marginalized. Put most simply, baptism has been reduced to something that happens to you once, rather than something through which you live every day of your life. Jesus himself, however, speaks of his own baptism as something he goes on living. 'Are you able to drink the cup that I drink' he asks James and John, 'or be baptized with the baptism that I am baptized with?' (Mark 10.38). We need to note the tense. He does not say 'the baptism that I *was* baptized with', but 'the baptism that I *am* baptized with'. His baptism gave shape and character to his life. It made him the kind of person he was. It committed him to a particular pattern. And that is what it is intended to do. Baptism, as Jesus understands it, is a state in which we remain.

The key to understanding baptism is to look at the significance of the water and at its rich imagery. Baptism is not, when circumstances allow, about sprinkling or pouring this water, at least only as a second option with which we have too often been content. Sprinkling water sparingly from a font the size of an ashtray says little about the generosity of God. The very word 'baptism' means dipping. That is the Greek – *baptisein*, the verb 'to dip'. Jesus was dipped by John in the water of the Jordan and the occasion has reminded people of a story where there was so much water that people talked of a flood over the whole earth.

So what does this water mean? The water of Christian baptism does not simply mean washing and cleansing. That is part of it, but it is not the part that the New Testament is much interested in. John's baptism was about washing and cleansing, but it was John's baptism that was being superseded by the arrival of Jesus with his new gift. You have to go to the Letter to Titus to find any biblical evidence on washing in relation to Christian baptism. The New Testament is much more interested in other images of water. For shorthand the Church has sometimes called these 'womb' and 'tomb', and font designs have reflected these concerns. The water of baptism speaks of new life, new birth and new creation. With a kind of breaking of the waters, we are brought to birth, and at Epiphany that is the natural emphasis. But it also speaks of death and of resurrection. For the Christian makes the connection between the great Israelite escape through the waters of the Red Sea and the journey of the Lord 'through the deep waters of death' in his passion and resurrection, and then sees in his or her own baptism a mirroring of both those events. This is what Paul is wanting his readers to understand when in his Letter to the Romans he asks, 'Do you not know that all of us who have been baptized into Christ Jesus were baptized into his death?' (6.3). And, if all that is not enough, there is the image of Christ as the Living Water that everyone who is thirsty may drink. Generous provision of water is appropriate for a sacrament with many layers of meaning, a setting where we encounter at work an extravagant God.

Even when our theology or our practice sells us short, that is what God is doing in baptism. With extravagant generosity he is joining us with Christ, giving us a new birth, setting us on a path of dying and rising, giving us his Spirit, all as we frolic in the water of his grace.

But even that description has something of an historical feel to it if we are not careful. It can sound as if that is what God *did*, once upon a time when we *were* baptized. But this insight, that comes out in the exchange between Jesus and James and John that baptism inaugurates a baptismal lifestyle, means we need to live out our baptism every day.

For Jesus, his baptism in the Jordan committed him to a life in relationship with a generous God, showering gifts. It committed him to a life where water kept being turned into wine. It committed him to a life open to the Spirit who dwelt within him, yet also came over and over again like a new gift ever fresh. Most of all, it committed him to a pattern of life and death and life again, a pattern of dying and rising, that reversed the world's wisdom. It was a pattern that defied the conventional and revealed glory where it was least expected. And all that can be true also for the follower of Christ who keeps reclaiming his or her baptism, though for ourselves we might add also it commits us to life in the fellowship of the baptized community and to life that keeps coming back for forgiveness and new beginnings, never falling away into despair.

Of course one cannot press the parallels between the baptism of Jesus and the baptism of Christians too far. For his baptism proclaimed his uniqueness. In a sense he was the first of many brothers and sisters, and we follow him into the water and share his destiny. That makes us sons and daughters of God, 'by adoption and grace' as the Prayer Book puts it. But he is Son of God in a way that is different. That perhaps is almost the clearest message of his baptism. It is why it is an epiphany. It reveals who he is. It is fascinating that twice in his adult life the voice from heaven acclaims him as the Beloved Son. First, it is in the baptism, which inaugurates the itinerant ministry, and, second, in the transfiguration that marks the end of that ministry and the transition to the focused pilgrimage to Jerusalem to complete his work on the cross. It is even more fascinating that a third affirmation of his Sonship comes not from the voice of God, but from the centurion as he dies, who speaks then for the human race, as he says, 'Truly this man was God's Son!' (Mark 15.39).

And that was the moment when he could most fully say, 'I have drunk the cup that I have to drink and I have been baptized with the baptism that was prepared for me.' This should not surprise us, for the cross, as much as the baptism, is an epiphany. It is another place where Christ's glory is revealed in our midst.

10

True host of the wedding feast

———➤◆◄———

The story of the marriage at Cana does not exactly complete the epiphany picture, but it is the third of the three great manifestations associated with the word 'Epiphany'. This turning of water into wine is a story that only John tells. It is rich in meaning, layer upon layer of it, some of it quite hard to get hold of, worth a lot of exploration. Unlike the coming of the magi and the baptism of Jesus, it does not have a feast day all of its own, but the story is retold every Epiphany, not least at Evening Prayer on the Feast of the Epiphany itself and usually as the Gospel reading on the Sunday after the Baptism of Christ. It finds its way into the hymnody, whether the fifth-century hymn of Caelius Sedulius, already quoted, or in Bishop Christopher Wordsworth's great Epiphany hymn, 'Songs of thankfulness and praise':

> Manifest at Jordan's stream,
> Prophet, Priest, and King supreme;
> And at Cana wedding-guest
> In thy Godhead manifest;
> Manifest in power divine,
> Changing water into wine;
> Anthems be to thee addrest,
> God in man made manifest.
> > (*The New English Hymnal*)

What are we to make of this story and, in particular, of its place here in the Epiphany season as one of the principal disclosure moments, revealing who this Jesus is? Full of rich meaning as it is, it is probably best to begin with the story at its face value. That is never enough with John, but it is a starting point. This was a party. Jesus goes to a village wedding. With him are Mary and his disciples. At this stage we are aware of six of these – Peter and Andrew, James and John, Philip and Nathanael. They share the joy of bride and bridegroom. They enjoy the party. Disaster – well, something little short of disaster – strikes. It will be embarrassing for the family, disappointing for the guests. The wine has run out. Let's not spoil the party, thinks Mary, Jesus will puts things right. There is a bit of reluctance on his part, for, as he tells her, his hour has not yet come. But he does put things right, in a spectacular way that leaves them with more wine, and best vintage at that, than they could possibly drink at even the most indulgent of wedding receptions. Whatever else it was or means, it was a party, an occasion of fun, pleasure, joy and celebration.

Here was a divine endorsement of festivity. A God who can plan 'a feast of rich food, a feast of well-matured wines, of rich food filled with marrow, of well-matured wines strained clear' (Isaiah 25.6) is essentially the God of the party, wanting people to be happy, to celebrate, to enjoy one another's company, the God of dance and song and even drinking. He is not a God to spoil a party. The presence of Jesus and his action at the wedding tell us that.

Yet what John most wants us to learn from the wedding at Cana is that it was a 'sign'. That is John's characteristic word and he prefers it to 'miracle'. It was the first of the signs that Jesus did, but he goes on, in his Gospel, to identify six more. There are seven signs, of which the triumph of the cross is the last. The point of 'sign' rather than 'miracle' is that John is not so much interested in what Jesus did as in what it revealed about him. What enthralled him were epiphanies, events that revealed who this Jesus was. He was operating as the only begotten of the Father, full of grace and truth, and they saw his glory. We are only a few hundred words away from John's prologue. 'We have seen his glory, the glory as of the only Son of the Father.' And they did – there in Cana of Galilee, Peter and Andrew, John and James, Philip and Nathanael did see his glory, and they believed in him. They saw, at least a little, what the sign meant.

But this could be too narrow an understanding of 'sign'. Certainly it was a sign that revealed his glory. That is exactly what John says about it as the story ends. But I think we need to understand 'sign' also to mean both pointer and promise. There were truths to which it pointed and there were promises it made.

The first is about marriage. If the story is a divine endorsement of festivity, it is equally a divine endorsement of marriage. The Marriage Service of the 1662 Book of Common Prayer speaks of a 'holy estate Christ adorned and beautified with his presence, and first miracle that he wrought, in Cana of Galilee, and is commended of Saint Paul to be honourable among all'.

By his presence, Jesus also commends marriage as part of the divine order for the creation. In an age when people do not always seem to see its point and sit light to its demands, it is important to keep affirming that marriage is part of what God intends for his creation and that it has the blessing of Christ. It has a sacramental nature and expresses something very deep about union and love. So much so that the biblical writers and the Church can never speak of marriage without drawing a parallel between the love of a bride and a bridegroom with the love of Christ and his Church. The key text, of course, is Ephesians 5.25 where Paul writes, 'Husbands, love your wives, just as Christ loved the church and gave himself up for her, in order to make her holy.' And he goes on:

> 'For this reason a man will leave his father and mother and be joined to his wife, and the two will become one flesh.' This is a great mystery, and I am applying it to Christ and the church. Each of you, however, should love his wife as himself, and a wife should respect her husband.
>
> (Ephesians 5.31–33)

This parallel that Paul draws enriches our understanding both of marriage and of the Church's relationship with Christ. He does not quite say so here, but the picture is not just of husband and wife, but of bride and bridegroom. Part of what reflection on the Cana story has done is to move very smoothly from the image of Jesus as wedding guest to the image of Christ as bridegroom. In fact in different texts the Lord is variously guest, bridegroom and host.

But the image of him as bridegroom comes from elsewhere in the Gospels. In Matthew, Jesus answers a question about why his disciples do not fast by saying that 'the wedding guests cannot mourn as long as the bridegroom is with them' (Matthew 9.15). Later he tells a story about the ten bridesmaids, five wise, five foolish, who await the coming of the bridegroom (Matthew 25.1–12). And there is no doubt who that bridegroom is. But the references are not restricted to Matthew, for John himself, just a little after the wedding at Cana, has these words on the lips of John the Baptist in discussion with his disciples:

> You yourselves are my witnesses that I said, 'I am not the Messiah, but I have been sent ahead of him.' He who has the bride is the bridegroom. The friend of the bridegroom, who stands and hears him, rejoices greatly at the bridegroom's voice. For this reason my joy has been fulfilled.   (John 3.28–29)

It seems that the Gospel writer himself wants us to move on in our thinking from Jesus as guest to Jesus as bridegroom. He wants us begin to understand that the relationship between Jesus and his followers is to have the depth, commitment and love that you see in a good marriage. And later, of course, in the Book of Revelation, the identification of the Church with the bride of Christ will be explicit (Revelation 19.7).

Out of this apparently simple tale of the village wedding is emerging a richness of insight. But marriage, whether about the relationship between a man and a woman or between Christ and his Church, is not the only sacramental meaning.

It is impossible to ignore the eucharistic layer of this story. John is the most sacramental of the evangelists. He is the one who wants us to understand that it is in water, bread and wine that we are joined to Christ and recognize him. But he does that, not by telling explicit teaching about baptism and Eucharist, but in a more subtle way, with stories of water at the well, bread in the desert, wine at the wedding, with hints of sacramental life that those who reflect on them will detect. The wedding feast at Cana, with its abundance of wine, transformed by the Lord, is clearly one such story.

So what happens if we apply three words we have used about this story – party, sign and pointer – to the Eucharist? The Eucharist as party is not a way people often think. Of course it is not just that, for it engages with life-and-death issues of the utmost seriousness. Yet Jesus invites his people to celebrate, to delight, to enjoy, to be in party mood and party mode. Sometimes the Eucharist can be like that, but we do a great deal too much hemming it in, so that there is not often much chance for a party to take over. Sitting in rows looking at each other's backs does not do much for party spirit. We need sometimes to look at how we celebrate (note the word) this sacrament to see that it really does become an occasion of fun, delight, pleasure and celebration. And, of course, a party is a gift with children, but somehow we fail to make it so.

The Eucharist is a sign of Christ's glory. As a sign it reveals who he is and the nature of God himself. It reveals something of both Bethlehem and Calvary. The presence of the Lord in the bread and wine that Christians share is a sign of the God of humility and simplicity who in Christ hid in the womb of the Virgin and took our nature in the baby laid in a manger. The presence of the Lord in bread that is broken into pieces and in wine that becomes for us precious blood is a sign of the God of vulnerability and compassion who in Christ takes away the sins of the world. In both, as we have been seeing, in crib and cross, he manifests who he is. The Eucharist is always a sign, an epiphany.

And then the Eucharist as pointer. It is the meeting point of time. It is the moment when the Church looks back to the Jesus who walked upon this earth and died and rose again. It is the moment when he is most deeply experienced among his people as they call down the Spirit to make the bread and wine and the community itself holy with his presence in their midst. But it is also the moment when the Church plays at heaven. It plays at heaven by daringly anticipating the joys of eternity. God gives a foretaste of the banquet of the Messiah, the supper of the Lamb. We take heaven, which in its fullness lies in our future, and we make it present, albeit only fleetingly and eclipsed by shadows of the earth. That is what Christian worship is all about, clocking into the life and worship and partying of heaven, which is where the glory of Christ will dazzle and delight more even than the signs we see on earth.

> You are the true host of the wedding feast,
> welcoming sinners to your banquet table.
> (Epiphany Acclamation, *Common Worship: Daily Prayer*)

In this talk of the future, yet another layer of meaning from the wedding at Cana is emerging. For, like the Eucharist, the marriage story is a sign and a promise of a heavenly reality. This is not least because the language that scripture and tradition employ about heaven is the language of marriage:

> Blessed are you, Lord our God, King of the universe:
> for the marriage of the Lamb has come.
> Make your Church ready, and clothe her
> with the righteous deeds of the saints,
> to join the praises of your new creation.
> (Service for the Feast of the Baptism of the Lord,
> in *The Promise of His Glory*)

This is an Epiphany text that builds on the bridegroom imagery in relation to the final chapters of the Revelation of John. Here the picture of the banquet of the Messiah, the feast that Isaiah had described in terms of rich food and vintage wines, has been developed into a marriage feast, where the bridegroom is the Lamb of God, the one who has taken away the sins of the world. The bride is the Church.

> Then I heard what seemed to be the voice of a great multitude, like the sound of many waters and like the sound of mighty thunder peals, crying out, 'Hallelujah! For the Lord our God the Almighty reigns. Let us rejoice and exult and give him the glory, for the marriage of the Lamb has come, and his bride has made herself ready; to her it has been granted to be clothed with fine linen, bright and pure' – for the fine linen is the righteous deeds of the saints. And the angel said to me, 'Write this: Blessed are those who are invited to the marriage supper of the Lamb.' (Revelation 19.6–9)

Here, we are at a village wedding, a very down-to-earth, and possibly drunken, affair; and yet, to the ear of faith, there are echoes of something like nothing on earth, a marriage feast in heaven. It comes at the right moment in the Epiphany unfolding, for we have moved on 30 years or more from the annunciation and birth stories where earth and heaven seemed remarkably close. Gabriel descending to Zechariah, Mary and Joseph, heavenly hosts over the fields, seemed to be saying that heaven is not far away. More than that, our understanding has been that in the birth of Jesus heaven has, in a quite new way, come down to earth and humanity joined with heaven. You could lose sight of that in time, but there is just a hint at Cana that that is still what this Jesus is all about, joining heaven to earth, creating a new union between God and humankind.

It is a subtle change from banquet of the Messiah to marriage feast of the Lamb, but it is not an insignificant one. It is partly that the anointed One is now identified with the suffering One who takes away the sin of the world. But it is also that the supper party of heaven is celebrating something akin to marriage. It is saying once again that the relationship between Christ and his people is to be understood in terms of the depth of union, of commitment and of love that marriage stands for. And, because it is set in the context of eternity, there is the assurance of its indissolubility. It is a promise 'world without end'.

There is one more theme to emerge from the village wedding. Like the others, it is a complex and subtle one. It is about transformation and new creation. One of the Epiphany Intercessions, as well as addressing Jesus as the host of the wedding feast, also affirms that 'you change our vessels of water into the gladdening wine of new life' (*Common Worship: Daily Prayer*). Here the picture is of a new and more splendid creation revealed in the water that is turned into wine. It owes something to Revelation 21 with its vision of the new heaven and the new earth, for the old have passed away. We are back to creation imagery, as we were with the dove swooping down on the water at the baptism of Jesus. The message is that, in the coming of Jesus, there is a new order and, lest it be thought that this is good news only for the Church, it needs to be emphasized that, focused as it is in the most natural element of the physical order, water, it is transformation for the whole creation. God is making everything new, everything rich, the material world as well as the spiritual. A wedding party is an appropriate place in which to make that point: 'In the water made wine the new creation was revealed at the wedding feast. Poverty was turned to riches, sorrow into joy' (*Common Worship*) says one of the eucharistic prefaces of Epiphany. The sense is that Jesus not only transforms the poverty of our human nature by infusing it with the divine, but that the whole creation is cleansed, changed and enriched.

Behind all the complexity of where God is at work – at the party, in the marriage, in the Eucharist, at the supper, in creation and in heaven; and beyond the different designations of Jesus himself – guest, bridegroom, host, lamb – is a truth that affects them all, and one that we need to hear. It is that Jesus is the One whom God sent to change everything. He it is who transforms the poverty of our nature by the riches of his grace.

There is that puzzling exchange between Jesus and his mother: 'When the wine gave out, the mother of Jesus said to him, "They have no wine." And Jesus said to her, "Woman, what concern is that to you and to me? My hour has not yet come"' (John 2.3–4). Despite that, he does what she asks and John finds rich meaning in what he does. But why hesitate, and what does he mean by 'my hour has not yet come'? It is something to do with the fact that this is only the first of the signs by which he will reveal his glory. And the ultimate sign, as we have noted, is the passion. And there the wine is transformed into precious blood. That is why the Eucharist, for all its festivity, is always focused on the cross, and it is why the marriage feast of heaven is the supper of the sacrificial lamb.

11

Follow me, brothers

The calling of the first disciples is not one of three great Epiphany themes. But the accounts of their calling feature early in the Gospels, all mixed in with the scenes at the Jordan, the first of the signs and the beginning of the ministry of Jesus where he appears proclaiming the good news of God. Because of this, these accounts nearly always feature in lectionary provision for the Epiphany season. Or perhaps there is a deeper reason. Perhaps the calling of the first disciples is a kind of epiphany.

There are variations among the Gospel writers. In Matthew and in Mark, Jesus has only just begun to issue his call to repent, for the kingdom of heaven has come near, when, as he walks by the Sea of Galilee he sees first Simon Peter and Andrew, fishermen casting nets into the sea, and calls them to follow him. Immediately they leave their nets and follow him. In no time at all he has summoned two more, James and John, who leave their father and their boat and follow him.

In Luke, Jesus exercises a lone ministry for a while. He preaches in the synagogue in Nazareth and in Capernaum. He heals a man with an unclean spirit and then a whole host of people, including Simon Peter's mother-in-law. So Peter is on the scene as an acquaintance, not yet as a disciple. Then comes a dramatic event on the lake, which leads not only Peter, but also James and John (no mention of Andrew), to commit themselves to following Jesus.

In the fourth Gospel it is Andrew, a disciple until that point of John the Baptist, who is one of a pair drawn to Jesus. He in turn brings his brother, Simon Peter. Next day Jesus found Philip and issued his by now familiar invitation 'Follow me', and Philip does so and fetches his sceptical friend, Nathanael, who is soon won over and indeed comes very quickly to faith in Jesus.

Although there are other differences of detail, as there always are in the Gospel accounts, the key variation is between Luke and the other three writers. In Luke's Gospel, the call of the disciples clearly emerges from an epiphany, a revelation of power and glory. They seem to have known already who he was. Certainly he was at home in Simon Peter's house and they knew he could heal. They may have heard him preach in the synagogue in Capernaum and they were certainly on the edge of the event when he taught the word of God on the shore of the Sea of Galilee, even if they were busy washing their nets. Then Jesus climbed into Simon Peter's boat, continued his teaching from there and then encouraged Simon Peter to put out into deep water and to let down his nets for a catch.

> When they had done this, they caught so many fish that their nets were beginning to break. So they signalled to their partners in the other boat to come and help them. And they came and filled both boats, so that they began to sink. But when Simon Peter saw it, he fell down at Jesus' knees, saying, 'Go away from me, Lord, for I am a sinful man!' For he and all who were with him were amazed at the catch of fish that they had taken; and so also were James and John, sons of Zebedee, who were partners with Simon. Then Jesus said to Simon, 'Do not be afraid; from now on you will be catching people.' When they had brought their boats to shore, they left everything and followed him.   (Luke 5.6–11)

This is certainly an epiphany experience. Jesus works a miracle. It is a supernatural catch. All are filled with awe. Simon Peter falls down at Jesus's knees as he recognizes that here is a man of power. The last people to kneel to Jesus, as Luke tells it, were the shepherds. But now it is the turn of the fisherman. He confesses his sin as he recognizes that here is a man of holiness. Jesus tells him not to be afraid. Simon Peter is the next one in the line of those who have heard that reassurance – Zechariah, Mary, the shepherds, and now Simon Peter – and this time the words are from the lips of Jesus himself. And, as with Mary, the reassurance soon gives way to the setting of a task. 'From now on you will be catching people.' It is a pattern that is repeated through the centuries. People come to faith and discipleship because they are brought to their knees by what they see of the activity of God, particularly in the death and resurrection of Jesus. Witnessing an event or hearing reliably of it leads to believing. As Luke tells it, it happens to Simon Peter first.

But, in this respect, Luke is on his own. The other evangelists present us with a slightly different picture, though the outcome is the same. For Matthew, Mark and John, Jesus does not have to do anything at all to win disciples, except to say, with disarming simplicity, 'Follow me.' It is not what he does, but the sheer magnetic pull of his personality and the gentle authority of his voice that has people abandoning boats and families and nets. As John tells it, the first six disciples are on board before Jesus does the first of his signs at Cana. They have become his disciples in response to who he is. And that, of course, is another pattern of Christian discipleship that is repeated through the centuries. It is when people grasp just who this Jesus is, the incarnate Son of God, rather than anything that he has done, that they come to faith.

One way or the other, Jesus is gathering around him a community of disciples. As we have seen already (in Chapter 8), the medium then becomes part of the message. The good news of God is a message about vulnerability and humility, has as much to do with failure as with success, and is a gospel for the poor. Jesus then recruits an interesting collection of followers, not many of whom look very wise by the world's standards, not many courageous, as it turns out, and certainly, as they lived the itinerant life with him, not many rich in the world's possessions. The good news for the poor is entrusted to the poor ones. This unlikely apostolic band is the model for the coming kingdom.

However, there will be transformation. The coming of Jesus brings that in its wake – transformation for the creation, but also for individuals. So they must change, the fishermen, into the mission partners of Jesus. It is people they must catch. The transformation is slow. It takes the dramatic outpouring of the Spirit at Pentecost for it to be fully effective. But the seeds of transformation are sown in the call to follow by the lakeside and they bear fruit abundantly when Peter and his fellow disciples begin to share the gospel of God when Jesus had been glorified.

There is in the calling of the first disciples another of those symbolic reversals of Old Testament calamity. It is another piece of evidence of Jesus as a new Adam through whom the human race begins again. Andrew, Simon Peter's brother, is the clue. But we need to go back first to Genesis 4:

> Cain said to his brother Abel, 'Let us go out to the field.' And when they were in the field, Cain rose up against his brother Abel, and killed him. Then the LORD said to Cain, 'Where is your brother Abel?' He said, 'I do not know; am I my brother's keeper?' (Genesis 4.8–9)

'Am I my brother's keeper?' It is a haunting question. In its context it is not a neutral question. Cain poses it with the expectation that the only reasonable answer is, 'No. You are not. How could you be?' Yet clearly God's answer is, 'Yes. You are. Your brother's life is inextricably bound with yours.' And, in a sense, the whole of scripture, all those books and all those words through many a chapter, are the answer to Cain's question posed in only the fourth chapter of the whole Bible. 'You are your brother's keeper, and your sister's too. Not in the sense that you deny them their responsibility and freedom, making them less than human, but in the sense that your life is joined with theirs. Your salvation and theirs is to be sought and found together.'

As the Old Testament goes on, brothers in conflict are a recurring theme. Although they did not often murder, as Cain did, there were tensions and the harbouring of grudges. They played each other false, even though, thank God, reconciliations – albeit in old age or after long exiles – were often part of the story. Jacob robs Esau of birthright and blessing. His sons all but kill their brother, their father's favourite son, Joseph, with his dreams and his many-coloured coat. But Jacob is reunited peaceably with his brother, and Joseph with his brothers, to the joy of the old father whose life has been marred from early days by family feuds. The Old Testament is a catalogue of relationships that go sour.

Perhaps it is not surprising that people who had so poor an understanding of the fatherhood of God should fail to comprehend its corollary – the brotherhood of humankind. For the one emerges from the other. A belief in a stern, distant, often merciless, tribal God suggests human relationships in which rivalry, cruelty and inflexibility will feature. But a belief in a loving heavenly Father – open, generous and vulnerable in his loving – might make for a quite different series of human relationships. From Cain's murder of his brother, Abel, the sons of Adam seem caught in a fallenness that drives us into isolation, separation and independence. 'No, I am not my brother's keeper; nor he is mine.'

The New Testament has hardly opened before a striking reversal is heralded. It is in the very first chapter of John.

> One of the two who heard John speak and followed Jesus was Andrew, Simon Peter's brother. He first found his brother Simon and said to him, 'We have found the Messiah' (which is translated Anointed). He brought Simon to Jesus, who looked at him and said, 'You are Simon, son of John. You are to be called Cephas' (which is translated Peter).
>
> (John 1.40–42)

Early in the Old Testament is a story of a man who killed his brother. Early in the New Testament is a story of a man who brought his brother to Christ. Scripture speaks of Jesus as 'the new Adam', the one in whom all the sin, fallenness and negativity of the first Adam are reversed. We might equally speak of Andrew as 'the new Cain', the one in whom brotherhood begins to recover its meaning.

The New Testament, by contrast with the Old, is full of brothers who live together in peace and harmony and do the Lord's work together – Andrew and Peter, James and John, Alexander and Rufus. More importantly than that, the New Testament witnesses an extension of the idea of brotherhood. Men who are not blood brothers trust one another as if they are. There is that marvellously moving moment in the story of the conversion of the apostle Paul, when Ananias, sent to Straight Street in Damascus, greets the fierce persecutor of the Church, the ultimate human enemy, now struck blind and led helpless into the city. 'Brother Saul, the Lord Jesus has sent me.' Brother Saul – what a greeting! No wonder, in years to come, that Paul so often addresses his fellow Christians in his letters as 'dear brothers in Christ'.

We are up against a linguistic problem. The way that language has developed, we now hear this talk of brothers in a very masculine way. It sounds as if women might be excluded. Nothing, of course, could be further from the truth. Not only is Jesus also followed by a group of women, but again he inaugurates a new order where, in a very male world, he gathers around him an itinerant community in which both men and women have a place. The difficulty is that we have no word in English to communicate brotherhood but without a gender implication. Yet, because the talk of brotherhood is thoroughly theological, not just a pleasant and endearing term, we need to hold on to it. It is not just about being friends or comrades. For the brotherhood of humankind is the consequence of the fatherhood of God. It is because Jesus taught his followers to call God 'Abba', 'Father', that they were able to recognize every man and woman and child as their brother and sister, for they are God's children too. He is their father. Andrew heard John the Baptist say that God called Jesus 'Son'. Jesus himself conveyed to Andrew and the other disciples something about living with such a broad and attractive vision of the fatherhood of God that they got the message that God's fatherhood, and the brotherhood that arose out of it, could not be restricted to family or tribe or country. I am my brother's, my sister's keeper, and every person is my brother or my sister.

So when Jesus invited his first disciples to follow him, the one thing that he offered, apart from himself, was a community. He did not offer a strategy. They were simply to follow him and find themselves catching people. But he did offer them himself, with all his pull and attractiveness, and he did offer them a community. People often talk about Pentecost as the birthday of the Church, but, in a way, the Church comes into being long before that. As soon as there is a group, first of men, later of women and men, following Jesus, living a common life, trying to discover how to replicate the family relationships of brothers and sisters in a new community of faith, there was the Church. Its beginnings are in Epiphany, rather than in Pentecost. It was as if they were in a new boat together. They had abandoned the old boats. But this was the boat of the Church and there were hopes of a great catch.

'Follow me' was the key invitation and they did and became themselves part of the good news of God. Sometimes it was 'Follow me', just that, not a word more, and something about Jesus made them leave the old world behind and join the new community. Sometimes it was 'Follow me and you will catch people.' There was a call to witness, a mission dynamic, and they responded. Later on, it would be a more demanding, sacrificial invitation, 'Take up your cross and follow me', and it would take them a long time to discover what that meant. Jesus said to Simon Peter, Andrew's brother,

> 'Very truly, I tell you, when you were younger, you used to fasten your own belt and to go wherever you wished. But when you grow old, you will stretch out your hands, and someone else will fasten a belt around you and take you where you do not wish to go.' (He said this to indicate the kind of death by which he would glorify God.) After this he said to him, 'Follow me.' (John 21.18–19)

That was a long way off, on the other side of the resurrection. But, even then, there was no strategy, just the magnetism of the one in whom the glory of God shone in their midst, and the simple invitation issued again, 'Follow me.'

CANDLEMAS

12

Carrying the light of the Lamb

The month of February has just begun when we reach the fortieth day from Christmas with a final incarnation story all of its own. For those who have long left all thought of Christmas and Epiphany behind, Candlemas must be something of an oddity, a strangely marooned feast, relating to nothing immediately around it. For those who have stayed with the incarnation themes through January, it comes as a climax, an ending and a turning point.

'Candlemas', of course, is simply a popular name, dating from medieval times, for the day properly called The Presentation of Christ in the Temple; though, as we shall see, it has other names as well. The event it celebrates is told by only one of the four evangelists, Luke, and he tells it in surprising detail. Nineteen verses are devoted to this story, which follows on in his narrative after the return of the shepherds, glorifying and praising God, and the naming and circumcision of Jesus on the eighth day from his birth.

Now, 40 days on, Mary and Joseph come to the temple for Mary's purification and for the child to be presented to the Lord, with the offering of sacrifice. There to greet them are Anna, the ancient prophetess (whose age of 84 we are given by Luke), and Simeon, who was 'righteous and devout, looking forward to the consolation of Israel, and the Holy Spirit rested on him' (Luke 2.25). On seeing the child, Anna begins to praise God and to speak about the child to all who were looking for his redemption of Jerusalem. Simeon takes him into his arms, speaks his *Nunc Dimittis*, and predicts that the child is destined for the falling and rising of many and that a sword will pierce the soul of Mary also. Mary and Joseph are amazed, but they do everything that the law requires before returning home to

Nazareth. We hear no more of Jesus until he returns to the temple when 12 years old.

The history of the celebration of this festival is a complex one. It is another of those many-layered feasts, with a host of theological themes with a claim to be part of the celebration – purification, judgement, presentation, waiting, meeting, light – to name only a few. Through much of Christian history it has been neglected. At its best it does three things. First, it engages with the Gospel story for the day, for there is rich material there to be explored. Second, it brings to an end a 40-day period of celebration. Third, it points the Church in a new direction and moves the focus from birth to death, from Bethlehem to Calvary, however long a journey to Good Friday, which could be as much as ten weeks away.

It is able to fulfil this third objective because of both the bittersweet content of the gospel and also because of the history of the feast which reflects that ambivalence. The story is an appealing one, very much part of the joyful Christmas cycle. The baby is there, the Spirit is at work, praises are sung and there is talk of light and glory. But there is a darker side, at least in the words of Simeon: 'This child is destined for the falling and the rising of many in Israel, and to be a sign that will be opposed so that the inner thoughts of many will be revealed – and a sword will pierce your own soul too' (Luke 2.34–35). Here is a prophecy of the passion and of the Mary of Sorrows at the foot of the cross. Indeed it may be a prophecy of rather more. In 'the falling and the rising of many in Israel' some have seen a prophecy of the Christian persecution of the Jews, reaching its dreadful climax in the concentration camps of the twentieth century.

Something of that ambivalence, the bittersweet mood of the day, was reflected in the liturgical practice of the Roman Church in the seventh century and beyond when, before the Eucharist of the feast, there was a pre-dawn penitential procession through the streets, carrying candles in the darkness. Later, as a code of liturgical colours established itself, the vestments of the ministers for this procession were purple, which underlined its penitential nature on what was, otherwise, a joyful feast. So the underlying hint of pain and conflict has long been there. Contemporary Church of England provision builds on this and ends the Candlemas celebrations with an explicit turning from the incarnation towards Lent and Holy Week. At the end of the procession, gathered at the font, the liturgy ends with these words:

> Here we now stand near the place of baptism.
> Help us, who are marked with the cross,
> To share the Lord's death and resurrection.
>
> Here we turn from Christ's birth to his passion.
> Help us, for whom Lent is near,
> To enter deeply into the Easter mystery.
> (Eucharist of Candlemas, in *The Promise of His Glory*)

Sometimes Ash Wednesday is only a few days away, sometimes more than three weeks. But the change of direction has been made and the Candlemas story has made it a natural transition.

We noted in Chapter 8 how Candlemas draws together one of the great truths of the incarnation, that the light for the world is in the coming of the holy, vulnerable one. For, after we have celebrated the stories that tell of the adult Jesus, who comes to the Jordan, turns water into wine and calls disciples into his community, we are brought back to the baby, not yet six weeks old. We discover the powerlessness and the vulnerability both in the young child and in the old man and the old woman who wait for him in the temple. We see the humility of Christ in his submission to the law as his parents do what it requires of them. And we catch a glimpse of the sufferings in Simeon's prophecy.

But there are other lessons to learn from this story and this festival. We may learn some of them from the four names of the feast – Purification, Presentation, Meeting, Candlemas.

'The Purification of the Blessed Virgin Mary' is the name by which the day has been most commonly known through most of Christian history in the West. It is a title that puts the focus on Mary, rather than her Son, and makes it a Marian feast. Luke's account is not entirely in line with the practice of the day. He implies that both Joseph and Jesus are part of the purification. Yet what the law prescribed was essentially a rite for women alone. Purification after a male birth, as laid down in Leviticus, comprised seven days of uncleanness and a further 33 days of house confinement, creating the

40 days after which the woman offered a sacrifice at the Court of the Women in the temple. This, presumably, is what Mary does. It is, as the title indicates, *her* purification. But Luke speaks of *their* purification. It may be that he, a Gentile, has simply misunderstood Jewish practice or it may be that, in order to create his dramatic story, he has consciously rewritten the scene a little. Yet there could also be a theological motive. Does 'their purification' suggest that what is going on is something different and broader? Is it the purification of the Jewish people as their Messiah appears among them? There are things to be put right, and here is the appearance of the holy one to put them right. The temple needs to be cleansed, purified, at his coming. Hovering in the background is the passage from the prophet Malachi that seemed to find fulfilment in this moment:

> The Lord whom you seek
> will suddenly come to his temple.
> The messenger of the covenant in whom you delight
> – indeed, he is coming,
> says the LORD of hosts.
> But who can endure the day of his coming,
> and who can stand when he appears?
> For he is like a refiner's fire . . . and purifier of silver,
> and he will purify the descendants of Levi
> and refine them like gold and silver,
> until they present offerings to the LORD in righteousness.
> (Malachi 3.1–3)

Mary comes to complete her purification, as the law requires, but it is the child she brings who is the purifier, not so much of his mother, but of his people and their holy place. Malachi goes on to say, 'I will draw near to you for judgement' (3.5) and the sense that Jesus comes in judgement on the old dispensation that has failed is present in this story. The old is judged wanting and needs purification if it is to be part of the new dispensation that Jesus inaugurates. As one of the Eucharistic Prefaces for The Presentation in *Common Worship* expresses it: 'On this day he appeared in the temple in substance of our flesh, to come near to us in judgement. He searches the hearts of all your people and brings to light the image of your splendour.'

So judgement, penitence and purification are part of what we bring to the celebration of this feast and they contribute to the bittersweet atmosphere it generates. But the primary title of the day in the West is The Presentation of Christ in the Temple. The focus is on Jesus and on the temple. Here again, Luke sits light to what the Jewish law actually prescribes. Custom did require the sanctification of the first-born by a payment, but not one necessarily handed over in the temple and not described as 'presenting to the Lord'. What Luke wants to do is to provide a dramatic occasion when the Lord comes to his temple and is recognized for who he is. The story has echoes, of course, of the presentation of the young Samuel in the temple in 1 Samuel 1. There can be no doubt that Luke is very aware of this parallel, for Mary's *Magnificat* draws strongly on the song of Samuel's mother, Hannah, when she leaves the infant Samuel in the temple, 'lent him to the LORD; as long as he lives' (1 Samuel 1.28). Whereas Samuel is left by his parents to grow up in the temple in the care of the old man, Eli, Jesus does go home with his parents, rather than stay with Simeon. Nevertheless there is the strong sense that he has been given, presented, to the Lord. When he returns with his family to the temple when he is 12, he comes out with that strange question to his mother, 'Did you not know that I must be in my Father's house?' Just as much as Samuel, Jesus is at home in the temple. Even more than Samuel, Jesus belongs to God.

This association with the temple is important. As far as the shape of Luke's infancy narratives is concerned, it is striking how the story begins in the temple with old Zechariah, who was 'righteous before God, living blamelessly according to all the commandments and the regulations of the Lord', and ends in the temple with old Simeon, who was 'righteous and devout, looking forward to the consolation of Israel'. It begins with a man who sings a blessing prayer at the birth of John and ends with a man who sings a blessing prayer when the Son of God is presented in the temple.

For Luke, it goes further than this. It is not just the infancy narratives that are enveloped in temple stories. When Jesus in the desert struggles with temptation, the temple comes into his mind. 'The devil took him to Jerusalem, and placed him on the pinnacle of the temple, saying to him, "If you are the Son of God, throw yourself down from here, for it is written, 'He will command his angels concerning you, to protect you'"' (Luke 4.9–10).

Later, in an act of purifying that his visit 40 days old had prefigured, he cleanses the temple, driving out the people who were selling things there and reclaiming it as a house of prayer. Through the week of his passion he was in and out of the temple, teaching the people. At the moment when he died on that dire Friday afternoon, Luke tells us that 'the curtain of the temple was torn in two' (23.45). For Mark, that rending of the veil marked the end of the significance of the temple and its replacement by the temple of the body of Christ as the house of prayer for the nations. But, for Luke, the temple remains part of God's plan and the focus of Christian ministry. For, in the very last verse of his Gospel, when the Lord has lifted his hands in blessing and withdrawn from his disciples, carried up to heaven, Luke tells us that 'they returned to Jerusalem with great joy; and they were continually in the temple blessing God' (Luke 24.52–53). They were doing exactly what Simeon was doing when the parents brought in the child Jesus.

So the title 'Presentation in the Temple' keeps before us some important insights. The temple, the purified house of prayer, is the place where Jesus and his followers are at home. Itinerant preacher and healer he may have been, pilgrim people they may be, but they are at home in the temple and expect to find God there. It reminds us also of the need to present ourselves, soul and body, to God in company with Christ, both now and at the end of time.

In the East they call this feast *Hypapante*, which means 'Meeting'. It is a feast of meeting. There is meeting that is real encounter in this story. The young couple, Mary and Joseph, encounter the old couple, Simeon and Anna. It is a meeting of faith, a meeting of generations, a meeting of the old world order, passing away, with the new world, just being inaugurated. Supremely, of course, for those who had waited patiently, it was a meeting with the Anointed One, for whose coming they had longed. In the power of the meeting, there was also a sense that all who were part of it met also with the Living God. For Simeon and Anna the encounter is the more rewarding for the years of waiting that have preceded it. They present us with a marvellous picture of patient holiness. Though Luke tells us little about them, there is enough to convey that we are in the presence of those who have grown so close to God that they can perceive what is hidden from the eyes of others. Their holiness has come of years of patient, yet expectant, waiting. Of them it can be truly said

We have waited on your loving kindness, O God,
in the midst of your temple.

(Psalm 48.9, *Common Worship*)

Waiting and meeting, they are part of the rhythm of discipleship. Life cannot be all encounter. Encounter there must be, encounter that changes things and changes those who meet. Neither Mary, nor Joseph, nor Anna, nor Simeon walked away from their encounter unchanged, and change, transformation, is part of what meeting with Christ always offers. But the rhythm also requires waiting – patient but expectant waiting – and for some life is much more about waiting than meeting. For Simeon and Anna the years of waiting were long, but the meeting that brought the waiting to an end was such a blessing that you can sense the near ecstasy of their praises.

There is a poem by T. S. Eliot entitled 'A Song for Simeon'. Eliot captures the sense of long vigil, as well as the foreboding.

Grant us thy peace.
I have walked many years in this city,
Kept faith and fast, provided for the poor,
Have given and taken honour and ease.
There went never any rejected from my door.
Who shall remember my house, where shall live my children's children
When the time of sorrow is come?
They will take to the goat's path, and the fox's home,
Fleeing from the foreign faces and the foreign swords.

Before the time of cords and scourges and lamentation
Grant us thy peace.
Before the stations of the mountain of desolation,
Before the certain hour of maternal sorrow,
Now at this birth season of decease,
Let the Infant, the still unspeaking and unspoken Word,
Grant Israel's consolation
To one who has eighty years and no tomorrow.

Grant me thy peace.
(And a sword shall pierce thy heart,
Thine also).
I am tired with my own life and the lives of those after me,
I am dying in my own death and the deaths of those after me.
Let thy servant depart,
Having seen thy salvation.

(*Collected Poems*)

But, for me, he fails to catch the ecstasy. 'My eyes have seen your salvation' (Luke 2.30) sounds to my ear like the shout of great joy of a Spirit-filled man. The meeting has been more than worth the waiting.

The common name for 2 February is Candlemas, and that might look to be a very simple name without much theological depth. It comes, of course, from the custom of carrying candles in procession, originally before dawn, though the custom has lasted longer than the early start. The logic of candles on this day lies in Simeon's words in his *Nunc Dimittis*:

A light for revelation to the Gentiles
and for glory to your people Israel.
(Luke 2.32)

Lighting candles is suddenly all the fashion in church and society, where once it was thought a superstitious thing. The symbol can be overdone, particularly where those who employ it lose sight of the truth that, in Christian thinking, the candlelight is always a sign of the Christ, the Light of the world. There is no avoiding the appropriateness of candles at Christmas, when we celebrate 'the true light, which enlightens everyone, was coming into the world' (John 1.9). But perhaps it is significant that in the Church's tradition a candle ceremony waits until the very end of the cycle and until the singing of Simeon's song that makes explicit the proclamation of Jesus as the revelation of God's light to the nations.

The stories have been piling up, glory upon glory, and now, right at the end, it is as if, through Simeon's song, we complete the picture. What does all this add up to? It adds up to the truth that the holy, vulnerable one, who reveals God's glory in our midst, is the light of the world. John could not resist letting out the secret in his prologue. Luke waits until the whole saga has unfolded and then spells it out on the lips of Simeon at the end.

Not, of course, that it is the end: only the end of the beginning. Simeon, remember, is pointing us in a new direction, towards the suffering and the cross. The Candlemas procession is not just about lighting candles, which people do a lot nowadays, but about carrying them, which people do rather less. There is something important in carrying. Mary carried Jesus in her womb. Simeon carried the child in his arms. Christians carry candles as a sign that they carry Christ into the dark places of the world. It is how they are gradually conformed to his pattern, whereby, eventually, they will, if necessary, carry not a candle but a cross and bring its light to the dark places of the world.

The cross and the candle are not very far apart. Simeon in the temple of the earthly Jerusalem carries the child, looks upon him and sees the lamb that will be slain and acclaims him as the light of the nations. Of the heavenly Jerusalem, John would write:

> I saw no temple in the city, for its temple is the Lord God the Almighty and the Lamb. And the city has no need of sun or moon to shine on it, for the glory of God is its light, and its lamp is the Lamb.
>
> (Revelation 21.22–23)

References

Atwell, Robert, *Celebrating the Saints.* Canterbury Press 1998.

Atwell, Robert, *Celebrating the Seasons.* Canterbury Press 1999.

The Book of Common Prayer 1662.

Common Worship, Church House Publishing 2000.

Common Worship: Daily Prayer. Church House Publishing 2005.

Coughlan, Peter, Jasper, Ronald, and Rodrigues, Teresa (eds), *A Christian's Prayer Book.* Geoffrey Chapman 1973.

Teilhard de Chardin, Pierre, *Le Milieu Divin.* Collins 1965.

Eden, Charles (ed.), *The Works of Bishop Jeremy Taylor.* London 1847.

Eliot, T. S., *Collected Poems 1909–1962.* Faber and Faber Ltd 1963.

Jennings, Elizabeth, *The New Collected Poems.* Carcanet 1986.

le Grice, Edwin, *Sharp Reflections.* Kevin Mayhew Ltd 1993.

le Grice, Edwin, *Sing Together.* Canterbury Press 1994.

Lewin, Ann, *Waiting for the Kingfisher.* Methodist Publishing House 2004.

Milner-White, Eric, *My God, My Glory.* SPCK 1954.

Morley, Janet (ed.), *Bread of Tomorrow.* SPCK/Christian Aid 1992.

The New English Hymnal. Canterbury Press 1986.

The Promise of His Glory. Mowbray/CHP 1991.

Silk, David, *Prayers for Use at the Alternative Services.* Mowbray 1980.

Ward, Benedicta, *The Prayers and Meditations of Saint Anselm.* Penguin Books 1973.

The Works of Christina Rossetti. Wordsworth Poetry Library 1995.

Acknowledgements

Extracts from *Common Worship: Services and Prayers for the Church of England* and *Common Worship: Daily Prayer*, published by Church House Publishing, and from *The Promise of His Glory*, published by Church House Publishing and Mowbray, are reproduced by permission of the Archbishops' Council.

Extracts from The Book of Common Prayer, the rights in which are vested in the Crown, are reproduced by permission of the Crown's Patentee, Cambridge University Press.

The extract marked AV is from the Authorized Version of the Bible (the King James Bible), the rights of which are vested in the Crown, and is reproduced by permission of the Crown's Patentee, Cambridge University Press.

All other scripture quotations are from the New Revised Standard Version of the Bible, copyright © 1989 by the Division of Christian Education of the National Council of the Churches of Christ in the USA. Used by permission. All rights reserved.

The two poems 'Wachet Auf' and 'Incarnation' from *Watching for the Kingfisher,* published by the Methodist Publishing House, are reproduced by permission of Ann Lewin.

The lines from 'A Prayer to St John Baptist' from *The Prayers and Meditations of Saint Anselm,* translated by Benedicta Ward, is reproduced by permission of Penguin Books.

The translations by Robert Atwell of passages from the fathers in *Celebrating the Seasons* and in *Celebrating the Saints,* published by the Canterbury Press, are reproduced by permission of Robert Atwell.

Acknowledgements

The lines from the poem 'Advent' and the poem 'Three Comings' from *My God, My Glory* by Eric Milner-White, published by SPCK, are reproduced by permission of the Friends of York Minster.

The prayers 'Come humbly, Holy Child' and 'Blessed art thou, O Christmas Christ' from *Bread of Tomorrow*, edited by Janet Morley, are reproduced by permission of Christian Aid.

The two poems 'The Annunciation' and 'The Visitation' from *The New Collected Poems* of Elizabeth Jennings, published by Carcanet, are reproduced by permission of David Higham Associates Ltd.

The hymn 'Sing with me a song of gladness' by Edwin le Grice, published by the Canterbury Press, is reproduced by permission of Betty le Grice.

The poem 'Kenosis' from *Sharp Reflections* by Edwin le Grice is reproduced by permission of Kevin Mayhew Ltd, Buxhall, Stowmarket, Suffolk IP14 3BW.

The lines from the two poems 'The Journey of the Magi' and 'A Song for Simeon' from *Collected Poems 1909–1962* by T. S. Eliot are reproduced by permission of Faber and Faber Ltd.

The Society for Promoting Christian Knowledge (SPCK) was founded in 1698. Its mission statement is:

To promote Christian knowledge by

- **Communicating the Christian faith in its rich diversity;**

- **Helping people to understand the Christian faith and to develop their personal faith; and**

- **Equipping Christians for mission and ministry.**

SPCK Worldwide serves the Church through Christian literature and communication projects in over 100 countries, and provides books for those training for ministry in many parts of the developing world. This worldwide service depends upon the generosity of others and all gifts are spent wholly on ministry programmes, without deductions.

SPCK Bookshops support the life of the Christian community by making available a full range of Christian literature and other resources, providing support for those training for ministry, and assisting bookstalls and book agents throughout the UK.

SPCK Publishing produces Christian books and resources, covering a wide range of inspirational, pastoral, practical and academic subjects. Authors are drawn from many different Christian traditions, and publications aim to meet the needs of a wide variety of readers in the UK and throughout the world.

The Society does not necessarily endorse the individual views contained in its publications, but hopes they stimulate readers to think about and further develop their Christian faith.

For further information about the Society, visit our website at *www.spck.org.uk* or write to:
SPCK, 36 Causton Street,
London SW1P 4ST, United Kingdom.